6 $\frac{95}{}$

87 prairie poems by Barbour, Bowering, Brewster, Geddes, Kroetsch, Mandel, Marty, Newlove, Stevens, Suknaski, Waddington and Zieroth

Poems that need to be shared, that keep on returning, poems that invite the reader to create his own memories, tell his own stories

TWELVE PRAIRIE POETS

Edited by Laurence Ricou

ISBN 0 88750 204 0

Design: Michael Macklem

Printed in Canada

PUBLISHED IN CANADA

For my father and mother

INTRODUCTION

The world when I began to know it had neither location nor time, geography nor history—Wallace Stegner, *Wolf Willow*

A good friend of mine, who otherwise has little interest in poetry, has a copy of Dale Zieroth's "Glenella, Manitoba" on the bulletin board in his study. I suppose Bob and I both discovered through that poem something half humorous, half desperate about our own growing up in a smaller prairie city, somehow removed from the centre of things. "Glenella" may be a subtle and intricate poem but it can be readily understood, it communicates its basic insight after one reading. Like most of the poems in this anthology it is a poem to be comfortable with, a poem which seems familiar and friendly.

My friends and I grew up in almost the same world as Wallace Stegner; it's probably because our world "had neither location nor time" that the poems now seem so important. Certainly these are poems to which the reader will often say: "that's the way it was." And, of course, in recreating his past the poet often depends on the details of location, as Zieroth startlingly, if indirectly, calls to mind the landscape in remembering his "Prairie Grade School":

> I was here on the day
> things first changed, the day I hid from friends
> who learned to play without me, discovering

5

I controlled nothing and growing afraid
for the first time of ordinary trees. . .

In moving, in that poem, from silence to a fear of trees, to a landmark that seems
tentative, even as a personal symbol, Zieroth suggests a sense of vastness more
effectively than if he had described it directly. But the memories—of the hushed
inviolability of the classroom, of the "new swear words," of the "rules" ironically
"intended to last for life"—are central. "Seldom, anywhere," notes Wallace
Stegner, "have historical changes occurred so fast. . . the Plains frontier in a cap-
sule, condensed into the life of a reasonably long-lived man." The remark begins
to explain the preoccupation with history but it doesn't capture the flavour of the
poems. The poets usually express a very personal sense of history—not a history
of monuments and buildings and long ages gone by, but a history of people dis-
covered anew, as if its existence is being recognized for the first time.

I began work on this anthology as a text for a course in Prairie Regionalism;
as I finish it I realize that this emphasis on a personal and human history makes
it a collection not only for careful study but for relaxed reading. I looked for
poems that would show the quality and variety of prairie poetry, and especially
for poems that both create and depend upon a sense of the locale and history of
the Canadian prairie, however unscientifically that region is defined by the poems
as a group. "Create" is the key word here: whether these poems are accurate
pictures of places or people is not especially relevant; the fertile questions are
how the poet has created the region through language, and what details of the
region he has used to reveal the universal. I believe that all twelve poets could
share the epigraph to Gary Geddes' *Snakeroot*: "Local colour is not, as the paro-
dists, the localists, believe, an object of art. It is merely a variant serving to locate

the acme point of white penetration. (William Carlos Williams)" I don't intend the term prairie poet, then, to be limiting in the sense that it describes poets who are sentimental escapists, or who are so caught up with prairie that they can write of nothing else. On the contrary, each of these poets explores a broad range of other experiences and images in his or her poetry.

In each case, though, the prairie is a prominent, and often persistent, focus of the poet's work. When the reader has the same focus I think he will find the impression more mellow and more positive than he anticipated. Certainly when I surveyed Canadian prairie fiction in *Vertical Man/Horizontal World* I found the land described generally as bleak and intimidating. Frederick Philip Grove's famous description of prairie song as "a vast melancholy utterance cadenced within a few octaves of the bass register" seemed quite suitable. But the songs collected here resist such classification by breaking out of melancholy into a hesitant, then ironic, and sometimes exuberant joy. Part of the explanation lies, no doubt, in the nature of the lyric itself: the poem is highly selective, likely to isolate and linger over a small detail and to concentrate on a specific, limited feeling or discovery. So, when Sid Marty describes an abandoned farm in "The Prairie," "the politics of wind/and money" is secondary; the poet concentrates on a crabapple tree, planted in hope years before, as an emblem of the mingling of married love, sensuous love, and love of the land:

> Crabapples cured by frost taste sweet
> tasting of cool nights
> moonshine cider,
> water, the depths of earth.

There is the "flavour of love," too, in George Bowering's delight with Alberta in "mud time," or in Miriam Waddington's childhood memory of the "Things of the World":

> The good things of the world
> she learned long ago
> from the sun   out there
> in the prairies   in that light.

Waddington's poem ends, though, by questioning the effect of "a blazing inno-cence" upon the "north Winnipeg girl," holding in check the natural tendency of memory to sentimentalize and idealize.

This feeling of love for the prairie emerges most convincingly in the poets' attention to people. Anne Szumigalski has written about her response to the prairie in a way which perhaps explains the number of character portraits in this anthology:

> In the end I think it is the sense of community that I found in Saskatchewan rather than the sense of space and isolation that has most influenced my work . . . I suppose, that in a place of great spaces and few people, every person is more important than he is in the crowded countries of the Old World.

Remembering or discovering a grandfather is, for instance, a familiar way of sinking roots both in location and time. In "Visions of My Grandfather" Douglas Barbour tries to place himself by exploring the connections among the facts of his grandfather's life, the vision of the prairie in his grandfather's paintings, the view from an airplane and his own poetry:

> & how i speak to you grandfather, of you for you   is different, a
> nother way,   these new lines long lines,   lean like the prairie toward
> some meaning surely some horizon far off   my eyes on
> your prairie, here,   or on your canvases/the thin lines of the plough converge
> toward a centre, vanishing point, point of the poem

Barbour rambles through shifting patterns of emotion and thought, attempting to establish his grandfather's significance. In this section (No. 9) from a much longer poem he ends in humble admiration, yearning for the love and innocence of his grandfather's time and place and art: "you saw it as i would have wanted/ & my lines stretch out to say so." Sid Marty's lines stretch out with the same yearning for his grandfather in "Now that the Clouds Are Gone Again." The poem is a poignant expression of regret that he had never shared his poems with his grandfather, for Marty realizes after his grandfather's death that both of them were makers of intoxicated, "rasping," primitive music which sang the song of the land: "the last time I held/those long fingers/I did not know that music/ pulsed from blood to blood." Marty's song catches both the slightly remote magic of grandfathers and the intuition that the grandfather is the limit for spontaneous, spoken connection with one's history.

By contrast Dale Zieroth's pair of poems to his grandfather is more of a bitter social comment than a discovery of a revitalizing ancestry. In "120 Miles North of Winnipeg" the abrupt and understated sentences penetrate to the man's quiet suffering and contentment. "Detention Camp, Brandon, Manitoba" describes the change in a proud man caused by a foreign war and a bigotry blind to individual human lives. Still with a restraint that is the poem's most moving feature, Zieroth builds a series of contrasts which tell how a man's spirit was drained and de-

9

stroyed: "Sunsets big/as God" in the first poem become but "a way/of counting days" in the second; the "leaving" which was unthinkable in the first poem becomes his overwhelming obsession in the second.

As the poems by both Marty and Barbour suggest, the prairie poet's memory often concentrates on dreamers and men of imagination. Robert Kroetsch, for example, combines details from *In Search of Myself* and *Over Prairie Trails* in his personal search for the essence of Frederick Philip Grove, prairie essayist and novelist. For me Kroetsch's Grove becomes the representative prairie writer, "the hobo tragedian," alone, struggling against the elements and the difficulties of language and form, who, when he finally reaches his destination, is greeted with nothing but an unknowing banality. Like the Earl of Southesk in Sid Marty's "Saskatchewan and the Rocky Mountains (1859–1860)," he seems to be valued mainly for his "wanton naïveté," for the things he "left unsaid."

And as for the things that are left unsaid: neither Grove nor Southesk is permitted more than a few words of his own. Few of the poems in the gallery of prairie portraits attempt the voice of the character: the poems are descriptive rather than dramatic. They seem not to be touched by the sense of experiencing characteristic of the dramatic monologue. Perhaps the poets are acknowledging the tradition of the laconic, inarticulate prairie man. Certainly a dominant note in the several poems for fathers is a terse rigidity, a reserve which governs even the closest of human relationships. In "Thirty Below," for example, Elizabeth Brewster recalls her father when she sees a distant, anonymous, and "solitary man" walking in a blizzard. The poet hints that her father, too, was distant and anonymous, and that only now does she regret having appreciated him so little when he was alive. Similarly Robert Kroetsch recalls in "Stone Hammer Poem" his retired father's absolute loneliness:

He was lonesome for his absent
son and his daughters,
for his wife, for his own
brothers and sisters and
his own mother and father.

And Dale Zieroth, in a poem titled simply "Father," recalls his father's gestures and actions, not his words; but the father who "shook/me like a sheaf of wheat" becomes more generous and contented at the end of his life. Recognizing this change leads Zieroth to an unexpected insight: his father has discovered a new stubborn courage in his own convictions and in the value of his own life.

Slightly more accessible fathers are found in Miriam Waddington's "A Man is Walking" and Andrew Suknaski's "Homestead," although the former appears only in a dream vision and the latter is "bent. . . thin as a grasshopper" by years of fighting prairie storms. Meeting Andrew Suknaski Sr., with "a binder-twine/ holding up his old wool pants," makes the prairie seem more human; Suknaski makes the point by specifying the homestead—section, township and range—in the title and then hardly mentioning the farm in the poem. The tender humour in Suknaski's portrait of his father threads its way through many of the poems in this collection. Not that the poems are likely to cause much rollicking laughter, but a witticism, or an incongruous detail often leads to a bemused and under-standing contemplation of human foibles. I find this view particularly evident in poems about the people of the small towns: for example, in John Newlove's wry comment on the fertility of Kamsack, or in Miriam Waddington's extended com-parison of the "Ukrainian church" and the prairie barn which ends with her tribute to the "little father['s]" wonderfully naïve prayer:

> let me hear
> how you beseech
> for all your people
> a clear road   an
> open gate and
> a new snowfall
> fresh   dazzling
> white as birch bark.

Suknaski honours a quite different priest in "Teo's Bakery." In the Breadbasket of the World the small-town baker seems to take on peculiar significance. As he describes Teo's drunken puzzlement and nostalgia he begins to see the baker presiding at a universal communion:

> lonely as judas i stop to watch teo
> thru the bakery window
> as he kneads dough like watered-down visions
> of childhood   suddenly
> he reaches for something under the huge table—
> my God!   teo!   a crock of wine—
> wine red as the sun pouring its warmth
> across the other side of this hungry world—

The central Christian ritual emerges in its primitive, natural ecstasy and a lonely, harassed small-town baker becomes a spiritual leader. Read closely, the poem gives rise to multiplying and deepening meanings, yet I suspect that Suknaski, like most poets in this anthology, would want to emphasize the basic character portrait. The simple language, the colloquial idiom and syntax, the hesitations, the parentheses, all insist on the primacy of the immediate subject.

The same is true of Robert Kroetsch's "Elegy for Wong Toy" where small-town puritanism and prejudice, or the speaker's own sexual initiation, are secondary to the affectionate remembering of Charlie: "You were your own enduring winter," Kroetsch tells him, thus rooting him in place and time. Again, as in Suknaski's "Teo," the poet's memory discovers some dryly amusing incongruities: Charlie's real name can only be found on a cheap calendar "above the thin pad of months,/under the almost naked girl." The final unlikely picture of Charlie seated behind "the heart-shaped box of chocolates" reveals not only the empty sentimentality of the town, but the torment of a man who is unloved, and, ironically, the charity of a man who loves all.

The farm poems, too, have this restrained comic note, as in Dale Zieroth's contemplation of the cycles of rural sexuality in "Manitoba Poem," the ticklish mice that plague Kroetsch's "Spring Harvest" or Gary Geddes's description of the cellar which serves as a makeshift toilet in the winter. Here, amidst oozing light, "green mould," and bottles of "blood," Geddes jokes about his own obsession with memory: "What is this impulse/to preserve, to set/this down?"

The impulse to preserve an image of the prairie's people often focuses, usually much more seriously, on the native people. Robert Kroetsch's prose-poems, "Old Man Stories," reinvent the Blackfoot legends of the Trickster. In "Indian Summer" George Bowering knows that the attempt to preserve the Indian past is an act of extinction, yet that, ironically, it may be in their death struggle that the Indians are most alive, like the river's continued pulsing beneath the ice. Geddes, too, feels a sense of unease that the Indian boys have little interest in the past that so absorbs him: instead they dream a more exotic history as "Lawrence of Saskatchewan." In "Like a River" John Newlove encompasses both the similarities and the distances between the white man and the native. Contrasting his own moving across the prairie by plane with the Indians' movement by foot and on horseback Newlove is led to question his sense of place and time:

How many signs must be known, how many curves recalled
to prove the traveller's still on the earth he thinks he is?

The answer, however, seems to lie less in the number of signs than in the nature of the search. Both white and native are nomadic, but the wandering has different purposes: the native's search is collective, for food; the white man's search is resolutely individual and solitary, for "rest and ownership." Consequently, unlike the fusion of races and myths in Newlove's *tour de force* "The Pride," the poem ends with the disappearance of plane and traveller, while the Indian wanderer and owner presides:

And on the prairie
the ghosts who own it continue to walk in clans,
searching for food and for what they once knew.

Brian Henderson, in a recent issue of *Essays on Canadian Writing*, noted the contemporary immediacy of these ventures into the past: "memory functions for Newlove as the imagination does, drawing resemblances, but through time, an aspect of process the present moment is always the end of."

The memory/imagination is active throughout these poems drawing resemblances not only as they colour the people of the region, but also more generally as they point a regional feeling, or an aesthetic, or a vision. Poems about space and flatness and restless movement, though no less significant than poems about particular distinctive people, are more what one expects in a book called *Twelve Prairie Poets*: poems, for example, like Peter Stevens' "Prairie." Stevens begins with prairie space to express a sense of man's relationship to cosmic space. The repeated "nothing" at the beginning of the poem is at once a reminder of human solitude, of the ultimate responsibility of the individual perception, and a challenge to insight: in a sense everything is visible. The prairie is the microcosm which seems to come to a definite end where the "sky sheets down" abruptly and the air is "glazed." But the eye can peer over the ledge, into nothingness, which is also the infinite space of the universe. By the simple device of splitting the preposition "in/to" Stevens suggests the range of possibilities. The "eye" and the "I" (the pun seems inescapable) open "in" or amidst space. They also open "to" space, and therefore to awareness and acceptance of it. And as they open "into" space the poet seems to see through space, and also into himself.

Many other poems play with such resemblances. In "Waiting in Alberta" Waddington finds the remoteness and the unusual June snow a narcotic that allows her to remove herself from reality and gain a new perspective on her world and her self. In "the oil" George Bowering links modern technology and the Indian past in a humorous account of "Alberta's unnatural heritage" and of its obliteration by a frenzy of Cadillacs. Douglas Barbour seems particularly interested in the relationship of words to the prevailing silence (a theme found frequently in this collection). "Poem: The Distances:" starts with quite precise images —"an uncoiled spring/a singing wire"—to express winter's cold space and the recurring cycles of life. But then the poem slips into seemingly more congenial abstractions:

Say only this, say only the hope
the urge expressed
in the movement outward the
sweeping gesture of construction;
and isn't this enough and
can't we say, and saying

                         comprehend
its magnanimity:

to whisper
across this frozen country
certain possible words

The poet reaches for articulateness, feels a hope, an urge, that will capture the
vast and yet generous spirit of the place. The abstraction "magnanimity" is a
fortunate choice, but it doesn't quite satisfy and the poem ends in ironic whispers
of words that have not yet been found.

Clearly the poems that concentrate on the physical space are more abstruse and
difficult than the stories of people. While small towns are represented by their
people, cities, like the open spaces, are seen as entities with little place for indi-
viduals. The city in Eli Mandel's "Edmonton, 1967" uses a precise super-realism
to preserve something non-existent. In a subtle way Mandel's Edmonton, at least
in its stuccoed neatness and its slipping into nothingness, is linked with the sur-
rounding prairie. Most of the city poems are still more explicitly linked to geo-
graphy. Sid Marty returns to Medicine Hat to find that "the sun is puzzled/by all
pretexts of a town." Bowering finds the "odd familiarity" of "the streets of cal-
gary" not in clusters of buildings, but in the "snow mixt with sand." Peter Stevens

describes Saskatoon as "living on the edge/of starvation's fact, dust's reality"; it is safe, but bleak and drained of imagination, of any sense of past or present vitality:

> We think we have cancelled out
> all possibilities of myths and legends

In this condition Stevens dreams, too, of the city's connecting with its primitive origins, of the waiting chiefs returning to

> invite the buffaloes back
> and dance,
> let off their own steam,
> call up their long dead legends
> and worship their gods
> surviving in their myths.

The dream, of course, as the work of these twelve poets shows, is general. The poets are seeking a sense of the past, trying to "call up" the "long dead legends," trying to establish the ascendancy of the imagination in an unimaginative world. In pursuing this, they naturally look to the oral quality of legend as a guide to their language and style. Repetitions, conversational formulas, simple colloquial diction, silences are commonplace. Indeed there is a nice harmony between the preference, in modern poetry, for spare language and open rhythms, and the prairie poet's most immediate subjects. An unadorned style, a simple landscape and the tradition of an honest, direct laconic people are neatly linked. Frederick Philip Grove suggested the same connection describing the pioneer homesteaders in *Fruits of the Earth*: "in their speech something hesitating, groping, almost deprecatory and apologetic; in their silences, something almost eloquent."

17

That description characterizes these poems with a startling exactness. George Bowering's "a sudden measure" is one demonstration of the insight that comes from a merging of minimalist poetry and a minimal region:

This sudden snow
   immediately
the prairie is!

Those houses are:
   dark
under roofs of snow—

That hill up to the cloud is:
   markt
by snow creeks down to town—

This footpath is:
   a bare line
across white field—

   This woman appears
   thru drift of snow:

a red coat.

The prairie is defined here by abrupt climatic change and, ironically, by whiteness. The houses seem to take their existence from their "dark" contrast to the surrounding snow. Further in the distance the "hill" has its presence "markt/by snow creeks" which link the receding landscape with the town. This image is extended as the hill runs "up to the cloud" and distinctions between land and sky are obliterated. The "footpath," evidence of man's presence and journey, would be hardly visible were it not for the surprise appearance of a human figure. The woman, unlike prairie, houses, hill or footpath, *appears*. The "red coat" without a body in it expresses a sense of apparition, even of magic, in the poem. But it is also the one bit of colour, the guarantee of presiding humanity, amidst so much white space.

"I'd like to write poems," says Gary Geddes, "that my family could understand." That's what a poem like Bowering's accomplishes; that's what makes it typical. The words are familiar and often monosyllabic, the lines are short, the pauses frequent: it is a poem that when read aloud would be readily understood. None of this, of course, is to say that the poem is not subtly crafted, or that it does not depend on the most careful selection of and respect for language, or that it is not rich with possible meanings.

If the poem can be read by the poet's family it implicitly makes a connection with the past: it links generations together and becomes, in itself, memorable. Perhaps only Eli Mandel's earlier poems do not fit with my comments about the verbal immediacy of the prairie poets. "Estevan, Saskatchewan" and "Prairie as Hawk, Cock, Belly, Lover" are more concerned with complicated mythological patterns, literary allusions, and ingenious metamorphoses than the perception of a small town or a landscape. But the extent to which these poems are exceptional is demonstrated by Mandel's own later works. "Narrative Poem," for example, is a model of restrained simplicity, in which the archetypal—and unfinished— prairie story is told through a stark sequence of cattle, shacks "and long/land/ and/land."

19

The same story is told more ebulliently in Elizabeth Brewster's "The future of poetry in Canada." By highlighting the "golden wedding anniversaries" and the "weather"—

People remember the time they threshed in the snow,
and the winter the temperature fell to seventy below—

Brewster acknowledges the value of the things so often celebrated by newspaper and folk poets. And the poem concludes (I recall hearing Brewster read these lines with a grin and a note of defiance):

I hope at least one poet
in the next generation
comes from Goodridge, Alberta.

I can imagine Elizabeth Brewster speaking here for all the poets in the anthology; she is also speaking of the many exciting poets, most of them young, who could not be included. I hope the readers of this anthology will become interested enough to go on their own search for poets who are remembering and telling the story of the prairie.

Meanwhile most readers should find here some bulletin-board poems, public poems that demand to be shared, poems that keep on returning, poems that are a natural part of the environment, poems that become embedded in memory. This book is made of such poems, filled with local and particular details and spoken in the casual, candid voice of a man remembering. They are poems that invite readers to create their own memories, to tell their own stories: I don't think the poets could want any better response.

CONTENTS

DOUGLAS BARBOUR

Born in Winnipeg, Manitoba, 1940. Spent many of his growing days on his grandparents' farm near Virden. His family moved east in 1954. Returned to the West in 1969 to teach at the University of Alberta in Edmonton. Books: *Land Fall* (1971), *A Poem as Long as the Highway* (1971), *White* (1972), *Songbook* (1973), & *He. & She.* (1974).

POEM: THE DISTANCES

Say only an uncoiled spring
a singing wire
                    stretched
across the deep white valleys
the cold, the seasons of
                            death:
say only this, say only the hope
the urge expressed
in the movement outward the
sweeping gesture of construction;
and isn't this enough and
can't we say, and saying
                            comprehend
its magnanimity:

to whisper
across this frozen country
certain possible words.

23

EDMONTON OCTOBER POEM

edmonton sky: a variety
of greys, tints
of executive thought, buffaloes
without thunder growing old.

this grey parades, pervades
thought, dulls
almost the landscape.

Yet trees shine, leaves
glow yellow, orange, red
on the bluff, blow

bright onto the swaying river,

crack the cold vision
in two.

24

SIBELIUS' AUTUMN

First fall day the grey
colour falling
over the whole ribbed sky
for miles, cold

air in a mass
thrusts across vast space
to collide with human faces,
tears on cheeks, red hands.

It can be heard:
a harsh rising resonance
of brown and yellow rushing
to corpses on ground and river surface
afloat, skipping
and drifting to destruction.

25

"lyre, even as the forest
is," your
harmonies rise
with that rising wind
sweeping across the prairie to tug
at our line of cedars, shove
them together swaying, their caresses
gentle even under the huge
sound.

This purely northern knowledge: today
I listen to his violin concerto,
something he felt because
the seasons made it clear
as only when they can hurt
they do.

The wind sings winter,
the violin a pure

white   frightening
in clarity, terrible

as the long snow, frigid
brilliance we shall know.

THE ACTS OF, THE MEN OF, TIME

A young man still, he
has painted the still mountains
while his daughters swam and played.

      Has heard a call:
and now, the occasion requires
integrity, clarity of vision.

The act was not flamboyant, flamboyance
did not enter; absolute
necessity dictated every move
(as he saw, clearly).

The act was
(in the image:)
a single coach
behind the huge black engine,
smoke gushing from the wide stack, streaming
out over the flat brown land
grain and hay rushing from horizon
to horizon to beat death.

27

These gestures
form our past
they make it
last though we
may pass them by
unknowing

(and my aunt says self
mockingly: your grand
father chartered a train
because mother was dying. She
always thought it was a whole train,
not this single coach, and
the huge engine straining
to make time)

the acts
of the past
are ours now

to claim
if we will
learn
of ourselves

heritage

Speed, speed, to rush, sweep
across these long fields
(stare out to the sharp edge,
the late light purpling
the whole bowled sky)

the fastest possible way
yet to fail
to see her again
alive.

Time, the price to pay,
she's gone, the act
was useless
we might say; and

   Yet the act was not
   flamboyant

   Just the pressure: discovery, of
   time, love laying claim
   to a long lonely journey
   through a land spilling in harvest
   to a covenant with death
   feared, and to be taken whole
   as life is, as our hearts
   take just what is offered, always.

IN THE FLATLANDS

Spring
spreads over the prairie
a huge blue sky:

    wide ranges of black
    loam, brown stubble

    frescoes:
    the burnished filigree
    of thin woods, bronze
    buds in trees
    occasional clumps of
    birch   (silver and tarnish).

earth falls away
on all sides, beyond
sight where clouds arrive,
begin their slow solemn cruise
overhead.

But eye and mind deceive
by making judgment:

grain elevators

rise behind woods,
sudden streams through
gullies, hump of bridge,
slight roll of meadows:

  perspective demands these shifts
  however minute.

Or a storm moves
on the flatlands,
across the distances:

  great cloud skeins untwine,
  windings
  drift with the wind diagonally
  down,   snarl
  on the rumpled ground.

  now, black
  where was blue and white
  before, the slanting fibres
  fashion muddy chiffon
  against a falling horizon;

to twine finally
with us: the image
lost

in the sudden swirl of water
drops as big as

the prairie hiding.

HOUSES

Flat pine, bare
grey often, and the empty
windows: these are
silent sentinels

out of the past,

          boyhood
sleeping in such rooms
beneath thin quilts, faded
linoleum on the floors

           (or
fifty years gone, the thin
flare of oil wicks, night
in Spring, ruts in deep mud
animal sounds by the trough: at sun up
all rise, biscuits
bacon, milk and the day
to plough, the heavy steps)

33

they are few and far
between thin lines of trees
to break the flat still spaces

                    (75 years
when Grandfather brought seeds,
saw in his mind
the inch of shade on a barren map).

We see the still houses,
they might be empty

as we pass.

34

VISIONS OF MY GRANDFATHER (NO. 9)

circling my intent   the facts
about you about which i know nothing
about which i go   circling

a plane about to land,   sweeping
once more over the runways   coming down   slowly
    to touch/solid ground

what i do know   what i can see/my
country: it was yours
                    differently
without these lines of civilized geometry   without
these smoky trails across the pure
                    the clear blue sky:

& i move deeper into this poem without thinking of how i'll get to the end.
naturally. i hope   & my prairie eyes move to follow yours   my
mind to understand.   the poem is new   & the poem is for you,

& how i speak to you grandfather, of you for you   is different, a
nother way,   these new lines long lines,   lean like the prairie toward
some meaning surely some horizon far off   my eyes on
your prairie, here,   or on your canvases/the thin lines of the plough converge

toward a centre, vanishing point, point of the poem
's endeavours i dont understand/i dont understand anything
but i recognize you grandfather   your great love for the land shines thru   you
knew it i know   & i do it i look at it too with new eyes because of you.

& that prairie i see in its lovely geometric patterns, stretcht out
to the end of the world you might think,   i might think
it stretcht to forever looking out across the patches from
our lowering plane,   seeing it as you never could, from
a thousand, three thousand feet in the air, & seeing
what you never could,   the grey straight strips of highway   lost
to points in the fuzz of distance;   you saw tracks gleam
to points, you saw dirt paths covered with wheat folded over &
you saw much less of man's ugly touch   your paintings
have that innocence   that you were artist   in love with the land
simply   not needing to make money off it   so you did not
need to sell it,   & with it your
self/lost to the land then the many who built it they thot
but you did not build i think you did not cut it up
into chunks of dead land we know too much of
too much has been done in our names grandfather & you
would not like it i think/sad not to have known
it could happen: i could live in it   look back at your innocence & wish

for it, for your vision of the growing land, land not yet patterned
so squarely, so that the slightly rolling prairie i see where you saw it
rolls uneven green & tan toward a sky untoucht by smoke

   from my descending height the prairie *is* flat
flat as a plate   it stretches until just before touchdown/slight
rolls of hillocks appear suddenly in/complete   flatness but against   real hills
or coulees running down to rivers   what we call
flat/prairie/the stretch of wheatfilld fields you loved in that season
of harvest   moment we worship   you & me   before
food, for flesh for spirit   that we might emerge in it
touch it & then see it/you saw it as i would have wanted

& my lines stretch out to say so   to spread the word across some paper
landscape to that horizon of questions for you my grandfather
having seen the answers   only answers i'll ever get   long before i began.

37

GEORGE BOWERING

Born in Penticton, BC, 1935. His father was born in Alberta; his grandfather was a circuit rider south of Edmonton. Was twice stationed in Edmonton while an aerial photographer with the RCAF. After teaching for two years at the University of Calgary, he published *Rocky Mountain Foot*, "a lyric, a memoir" of Alberta which, with *Gangs of Kosmos*, won the Governor General's Award in 1969. Books include: *Points on the Grid* (1964), *The Silver Wire* (1966), *The Gangs of Kosmos* (1969), *Rocky Mountain Foot* (1969), *Sitting in Mexico* (1970), *Al Purdy* (1970), *Touch: Selected Poems* (1971), *Genève* (1971), *Autobiology* (1972), *Curious* (1973), *Layers* (1973), *In the Flesh* (1974), *Flycatcher* (1974).

38

PRAIRIE

Smoke-stack in prairie sky
marks a city,
some group of men
intent on living there,

living absurd.
The topology
permits moss-rooft cabins,
tribe of prairie dog eaters.

Not commerce.
Even the river is tribal,
a wandering sludge:
no place for turbines.

The prairie
makes men brown;
they scratch the soil
or dig deep into it:

like prairie hens,
like prairie dogs.

39

THE OIL

Sleepy old mind, I'm driving a car
across the prairie shivering under snow sky.
Old sky: I suddenly see with one rise of road
old buffalo fields,

                  there is nothing
but buffalo turds on the grass
            from which we keep
            the home fires burning.

Alberta
        floats on a pool of natural gas
        the Piegans knew nothing of
        in their fright
        in their flight
          to the mountains.
                    We owe them that.

This straight line of highway
        & ghost wheat elevators
everything here in straight lines
        except the Indian fields,

                                          they roll
we say, rolling hills,
                              but our things are
straight lines,
                    oil derricks, elevators, train tracks
the tracks of the white man
                                        the colour of
no white man, but
                        dark as the earth
in its darkness,
                        down deep oozing things:
I mean oil.
              Alberta's unnatural heritage
concocted of Catholic adoption agencies
        & fundamentalist
                                    crooked coffee-stained neckties
    at the expense of Indian boys,
        now Catholics with horses removed
from under them,
                        the Piegans crosst the Rockies
to British Columbia
                        where oil is more scarce
& people.

41

       In the high trees they rise now,
with campfire smoke,
                      the smell of needles burning.

Buffalo shit smoke
                burning in Alberta
by the road, highway 2 North.

Now a
       Cadillac, I see a
               nother Cadillac, & there
is the black straight road, &
               a Cadillac,
                   two Cadillacs
on the road, racing, North,
             the mountains to the left
blurred by a passing
       Cadillac.

A SUDDEN MEASURE

This sudden snow:
   immediately
the prairie is!

Those houses are:
   dark
under roofs of snow—

That hill up to the cloud is:
   markt
by snow creeks down to town—

This footpath is:
   a bare line
across white field—

   This woman appears
   thru drift of snow:

a red coat.

43

INDIAN SUMMER

The yellow trees
along the river

are dying I said
they are in
their moment of life
you said.

The Indians I think
are dead, you cant
immortalize them, a
leaf presst between
pages becomes a
page.

In a month
the river will move

beneath ice, moving
as it always does
south. We will
believe it as we

will no longer see
those yellow borders
of the river.

If names are history
                here
     I offer mine
        to add two years
                    time told with proper
                    nouns

                    "In 1905, Alberta took shape
                    on the map of Canada; but
                    history was recorded on the
                    face of Alberta many years
                    before that."

                            I find history
                            is towns—

Medicine Hat, Alberta

                        where serpent told Cree
                        brave to throw
                        his wife
                        into the water

which he did
for power &
an old man's hat
to kill the Blackfoot.

(So history again
is death)

only to be wasted for

Wetaskiwin, Alberta

(where my father
was born)

& peace between
Blackfoot & Cree,

that is,
wi-ta-ski-oo cha-ka-tin-ow,

also
Peace Point,
Cheneka.

(or rather, history
is pact.)

High River, Alberta
Okotoks, Ponoka, Kananaskis, Kahwin,
Etzikom, Netook, buffalo tracks—

Bow River, for weapons & the white man

           & later his names,
           the oddments of his map

           made not from grass
           but paper.

           Proper.

Or it could be said:

           property,

           which is
           another name for
           history.

Which I cant expect to bring.

Other than that,

           I can name
           my wife
           & unborn children

           some other place.

48

PRAIRIE MUSIC

Some bugle blow
over these cold bare fields

phantom sound to meet
prairie night, this I

know has to be prairie sound
the music I heard that night

on Winnipeg highway
miles from the nearest light

the stars, a bugle blow
away. The loneliest place

Kanada, a place for Kanada
the great prairie, formerly

a colour picture in a
book about the country

lonely place, the black
expanse, waiting for headlights

the sound of an engine
the soundlessness of the night

where no bugle played
in that cold.

CPR WINDOW

For Raymond Souster

The night train
across the prairies

passes small villages
with their few trees

plowed snow of streets
& is gone again

into the next hundred miles
of dark snow.

50

THE STREETS OF CALGARY

The streets of Calgary
are snow mixt with sand,

what flies thru this air
to rest finally, chugged under

snow tires. This is the odd familiarity
of prairie town, not the camera's art

of clustered downtown buildings
in the distance, that calendar picture;

but the moving close-up under
headlights, the snow mixt with sand.

Later, in another city, you have
album pictures of downtown buildings.

You have to come back, drive at night
to know you have been here
                on snow mixt with sand.

COLD SPELL

Snow! Snow!
all over the city, blowing
between buildings, down streets,
up skirts, between legs,

encases my chest in cold grab
fingers at my heart
between my legs
up my ankles—

Memory mornings:
brushing snow off the car
7.30 in the morning
no wind, thirty below zero, ha-ha!

Snow! lying still
waiting boot clomp & tire squash.

Like they say Virgin Snow,
Pure as the driven snow.

Early morning snow shoveller
I am virginity-taker, deflowering ogre,
violation animal of wet gloves,
frozen nostril sniffer,
snow-squasher,
squeek-squeek of boots on snow—

Stay out long enough
& it needles in to your guts,
snow sifting in there
between liver & kidneys, lung & spleen,
freezing synapses, diluting blood,
leaving water-blood corpses under snow-humps!

Snow blowing on windshields,
blizzard road, main artery of the city
frozen solid, cars still in ice disbelief,
icicles on the ends of police noses
directing traffic red green red green:
no-one moves,

dogs frozen with legs up
caught in the act of pissing,
supported on yellow arcs of ice.

53

The northern lights frozen stiff, heavy,
fall in great crashes across Alberta,
flattening cities, making weird green mountain ranges—

The whole air
frozen solid,
The world a ball of ice....

A man
dont give a damn—
if the sun's shining a little.

54

MUD TIME

I like Alberta best
   with mud on the ground,

  Spring
       softening things,

  warm air
        that does not move.

All the cars
       have mud on them.

There is still snow
  on tree-shaded streets.

  But the very centre
  of my body
       has melted.

ELIZABETH BREWSTER

Born in Chipman, NB, 1922. Educated at UNB, University of Toronto Library School and Indiana University, where she did her doctoral dissertation on George Crabbe. Taught, and worked in the Library, at the University of Alberta, Edmonton. Now teaching at the University of Saskatchewan, Saskatoon. Books: *East Coast* (1951), *Lillooet* (1954), *Roads* (1957), *Passage of Summer: Selected Poems* (1969), *Sunrise North* (1972), *In Search of Eros* (1974), *The Sisters* (1975).

56

SUNRISE NORTH

Drawing my drapes, I see
pink and purple clouds of dawn
over the white-roofed city,
smoke in rising fountains,
the lights of early risers
twinkling far off,
the new moon, hanging low,
beginning to pale in the morning sky.

The beautiful northern city
is a child's Christmas toy
spread out like blocks
with here and there a tree
deftly placed
discreetly frosted;
and, like a child,
I want to pick it up,
move a house here, a tree there,
put more frost on that distant dome.

The colours fade, the pale blue sky grows higher.
Now I see the sun
gradually rising
over the rim of water-flat plain,
bonfire bright, triumphant.
Soon I shall walk out,
through the white snow, dry as sugar,
into the real street.

58

THE FUTURE OF POETRY IN CANADA

Some people say we live in a modern mechanized nation
where the only places that matter
are Toronto, Montreal, and maybe Vancouver;
but I myself prefer Goodridge, Alberta,
a town where electricity arrived in 1953,
the telephone in 1963.

In Goodridge, Alberta
the most important social events
have been the golden wedding anniversaries of the residents.
There have been a Garden Club, a Junior Grain Club, and a Credit Union,
and there have been farewell parties,
well attended in spite of the blizzards.

Weather is important in Goodridge.
People remember the time they threshed in the snow,
and the winter the temperature fell to seventy below.

59

They also remember the time
the teacher from White Rat School
piled eight children in his car
and drove them, as a treat,
all the way to Edmonton;
where they admired the Jubilee Auditorium
and the Parliament Buildings
and visited the CNR wash rooms
but were especially thrilled
going up and down in an elevator.

I hope at least one poet
in the next generation
comes from Goodridge, Alberta.

60

SUNDAY AFTERNOON, DOWNTOWN EDMONTON

Almost nobody stirs
in this concrete desert.
Sunshine burns
through the hot bright hazeless inland air
dazzles the eyes
and prickles the skin.
All the buildings look empty.
A few passers-by stare into windows;
a few policemen stand at street corners.
Men sit on shadeless benches
as though waiting for something to happen
which will probably never happen.
A dozen boys wait
for a bus which takes half an hour to come.
There is nothing to do,
and the afternoon is too hot
for doing nothing pleasurably.

61

YEAR'S END

On this pitchblack morning
of the last week in December
I sit by the train window
eating toast and jam,
trying to see out.

At Wainwright
there are lights in houses,
an electric Christmas wreath
flashing red and blue
from the front of the station.

Gradually shapes appear
buildings slide past.
The new snow is grey-green
in the half light.

Near the town of Viking
we sway past a dump
where cars and trucks
lie on their sides
half-filled with snow.

A pile of tires,
a clump of green tractors
lie under drifts.

Under the pale sky
the snow is washed with light,
becomes blue
tinged with faint pink
of the unseen sunrise.
Trees are like artificial trees
made of handkerchiefs.
In some fields the snow is ridged
becomes goose pimpled.
Brown grass stubbles the white.

Far off in one field
a red-brown horse moves
warm in the whiteness.
There is a red barn with a blue roof
there there
and there
is a black dog running.

63

THIRTY BELOW

The prairie wind sounds colder
than any wind I have ever heard.
Looking through frosted windows
I see snow whirl in the street
and think how deep
all over the country now
snow drifts
and cars are stuck
on icy roads.
A solitary man walking
wraps his face in a woollen mask,
turns his back sometimes
so as not to front
this biting, eye-smarting wind.

Suddenly I see my dead father
in an old coat too thin for him,
the tabs of his cap pulled over his ears,
on a drifted road in New Brunswick
walking with bowed head
toward home.

MUNCHAUSEN IN ALBERTA

Our first winter in the settlement,
the old man said,
January was so cold
the flames in the lamp froze.
The womenfolk picked them like strawberries
and gave them to the children to eat.

That's the only time
I was ever a fire-eater.

65

GARY GEDDES

Born in Vancouver, BC, 1940. Raised on the West Coast except for four years as a boy on a farm near Yorkton, Saskatchewan. Educated at UBC, Reading and the University of Toronto. Edited the valuable anthologies *20th-Century Poetry and Poetics*, *15 Canadian Poets*, and *Skookum Wawa: Writings of the Canadian North West*. After several years as a teacher and graduate student he is now free-lancing as writer and editor from Victoria, BC. Books: *Poems* (1971), *Rivers Inlet* (1972), *Snakeroot* (1973), *Letter of the Master of Horse* (1973).

66

PLAINS

after the calamitous
Rockies
          these plains seem
made for co-existence

smoothed by aeons of ice
and wind   separations
and returns

          they
are where life is lived
when we come down at last
from the mountains
             bearing
our unspeakable dreams

67

WILD STRAWBERRY

all this hardware
has engineered my coming,
higher than the crow flies
and straighter, the train
streaking through buffalo country
dust cloud of sleek Greyhound

behind in grey cities
voices of wood and wind
the willow-pipe, fragrance
of crocus and wild strawberry,
lost in a crash of metals

I am barren
before the spectacle,
a *tabula rasa*, nothing to offer
but the gift of my attention

my tendrils reach down,
spread like quack grass
in the familiar soil

LAWRENCE OF SASKATCHEWAN

I

All day scratching for arrow
heads in post-glacial blow-outs
near Battleford. The signs
of human history are few,
stones in a well.

Deer and Rabbit Skin, who
call me uncle and chatter
incessantly at my side,
know, too well, the price
of being what they are.
All the ceremonial dances
in Saskatchewan cannot
eliminate that knowledge.
But they are young, flexible;
they accommodate the pale
ghost who wanders in and out
of their lives, try to share
his interest in their past.

2

In the other room, edging
toward sleep, they are relieved
of their history, their colour.
Gift Moroccan daggers strapped
to their pyjamas, they dream
of white horses, flashing swords,
a camel caravan with me out front,
the Atlas mountains as backdrop.

I find only buck-brush
and ground cedar, some sage
and flowering cactus.

69

WINTER

Winter:

(the image is enough, is
somewhere to start from)

     the drill
of hot milk hitting the pail,
steaming turds that disappear
beneath the sleigh's runners,
the cold fingering howl
of coyote.

Here you are never far
from winter, it hangs
like an icicle in the mind.
Blank pages that begin
and end a story, whiteness
underlying the delicate
print of summer.

SNAKEROOT

Along the dirt roads of summer,
black prairie mud oozing my toes,

sun-baked ridges of clay
crumbling, the childhood me

scrambles for Senega root,
in ditches, edges of pastures,

along the road allowance,
staggers home reeling from sun,

no more than an ounce of rare
weed in my pocket, craggy

pungent rattlesnake root, a
smell the nose remembers.

The road to hell is paved. Along
its length snakes proliferate, wind

themselves about our lives, poison
the air we breathe. All night

the rattle of traffic, faces stare
from bloodshot windows. Somewhere

a root so potent it would cure
the sting of concrete and macadam,

hurt of steel, a burning in the lungs,
some magic elixir of leaves and sweet

grasses, essence of wildflowers, tiger
lily, gum of fresh, chewed wheat, free

to all takers, that will end the long
bitterness, mend the bruised heel.

THE ANGELS ARE IN A SLUMP

I

Switch on the radio.
The yellow needle glides
along its fixed track
from one community of sound
to the next. Music gives way
to hourly voices bringing
news and sport.

Slack-jawed Bobby ponders
a play for third. The game
is scrub, with mixed teams
and three men up. Eileen
squares her tight nipples
to the plate. The infield
shuffles. At short-stop,
Peter dreams of Molly, lifting
her skirts to heaven behind
the barn. The ball is hit,
a pop fly. It traces a thin
trajectory to Pete's glove.

The past is too certain, too
predictable. He will turn
and tag the unspeakable Bobby
for a double play. They will
wander forever in a limbo
between bases, strike out
on unexpected curves.

73

2

Slim fingers rifle
the files of memory.

I am in the schoolyard,
alone, standing among weeds
and goose grass, remembering
only my rememberings.

The past is no more certain
than the present, is something
dimly perceived, if at all,
something continually to be
edited, rewritten;
yet it is *there*,
the other country we inhabit,
inhabiting us, as these figures
perform their solemn dance.

Tune them out,
send the needle spinning
past notes and squacks and voices
into a field of silence.

74

NOON TRAIN

Writing these poems
I discover Lemieux's Noon Train
hanging in the capital.

The machine itself resembles
a rusting spike, driven
into the heart of winter.
Actually, it is no more
than a diminishing line of brown
in two grey fields, the grey
of sky a shade or two darker
than the grey of February snow.

The canvas depicts a freight
disappearing into a pin-hole
in the horizon, while two frail
divisions of trees stop short,
seeming to retreat or fall back
before this infernal engine.

The tension in these
lines of force, these areas
of almost colour, confounds me.
The economy of art and nature,
no frills.

CANNING

Canning saskatoon berries,
188 quarts in a summer.

Above me voices, slap of cards,
feet shuffling over linoleum,
the crackle of wood fire.
Those were clever tricks,
sluffing off the queen of spades
on grandmother, farting silently
in the kerosene gloom.

76

Light oozes cracks
of trap-door, covers beams
and rough scaffolding.
Turnip faces hunch and stare
in the dank root cellar, quarts
of dark blood line the shelves.
Green mould in the jar
nearest me, more voices,
click of knitting needles.
Robespierre on the pot,
knees trembling, bowels locked,
not fearing death, but only
the indignity of constipation.

What is this impulse
to preserve, to set
this down?

77

ROBERT KROETSCH

Born 1927, Heisler, Alberta. Studied at the University of Alberta, Middlebury College and State University of Iowa. Worked in the North from 1948 to 1954. In 1961 began teaching English at State University of New York, Binghamton. His novel *The Studhorse Man* won the Governor General's Award in 1969. Books: *But We Are Exiles* (1965), *The Words of My Roaring* (1966), *Alberta* (1968), *The Studhorse Man* (1969) *Gone Indian* (1973), *The Ledger* (1975), *The StoneHammer Poems* (1975), *Badlands* (1975).

Old Man, one evening, came to the Sun's lodge, and was invited to stay for a visit. In the morning the two men went hunting. The Sun put on leggings bright with porcupine quills and eagle feathers. He ran around a patch of bush and the bush burst into flame: out ran two white-tailed deer and a bull moose.

That night Old Man stole the leggings. He went out into the darkness, leaving no word for his host, and he walked far down the Oldman River, down into a coulee, before wrapping himself in his robe. In the morning he was awakened by a voice. "Get up, Old Man, your venison is ready." Old Man opened his eyes; he was in the Sun's lodge.

That night he stole the Sun's fire-leggings again. He sneaked away from his blankets; he ran across the prairie; he fell down into a buffalo wallow and got up and ran again, following a buffalo trail; he ran until, exhausted, he fell down into sleep. In the morning he was awakened by the Sun. "Excuse me," the Sun said. "But you are lying on my leggings, Old Man."

"Ha," Old Man said. "They seem to follow me around. Maybe they like me." "Then they are yours for the taking," the Sun said. "But remember they are medicine leggings. Wear them only when you go out to hunt."

79

Old Man came to the camp of some Piegans. He saw the beautiful Piegan women. He went into a lodge and put on his splendid leggings, decorated with porcupine quills and eagle feathers.

At his first step they burst into flame. He began to run. The grass caught fire. He ran faster. "You are trying to burn us up," the Piegans cried in anger. Old Man ran all morning, ran all afternoon. At evening he came to a river. He jumped in. The leggings fell off in black pieces.

OUTSIDE MOOSE JAW:
A WHIRLWIND: SILENCE

Is where old men kick and gather
Empty beer bottles in dry ditches;
Old men pick penny wealth from bulrush
And foxtail, from rosebush and thistle
And alkali dust:
                     while quick on the hot
Horizon—a tower of teasing wind
Tumbles a crow out of its black pride,
Hurls haystacks up to chaos and swings
A cat of straw.
               Is where God writes
On the walls of icicled barns,
On a cold and granite boulder
Promising that JESUS SAVES
The spring wheat lining the black field green,
The mare in foal weary for tall grass
And the new sun, and heads of barley
Wanting for one filling rain:

Is where old men kick and gather
Empty beer bottles in dry ditches.

81

SPRING HARVEST

I

That fall   we were snowed in
while the grain stood in stooks

and all winter long the mice
multiplied in the stooks   the owls

came to the drifted fields
as if the white North was emptied

of owls   as if Kenojuak herself
had created   their pitiless eyes.

2

One teamster was too proud   that spring
to tie his pant legs shut; I saw him
swatting at his balls as if
his prick itself had turned   into a mouse.

My aunt   cooking for threshers
(and scared to death of mice)
noticed a wisp of smoke,
told me to climb the windmill.

And looking out squint-eyed from my perch
over that circle of prairie and slough hole,
I saw the flames (like a plague of red
mice) coming north under a south wind.

83

3

We were half blind
in the smoke, swatting
with wet sacks,
the flames leaping
each fire line   before
it was ploughed
wide enough
or black;
              the earth
and sky   hinged
on a red
tongue
as if   we had ourselves
been snatched up,
would be devoured.

4

The flames harvested that crop.
The owls must have gone
back North on the south wind.
The men, forgetting their dreams,
got on with the spring sowing.

But I remember those owls
at night   on the silent snow
and the fat mice   squealing
out of the flames   as if
each stook   was a burning bush.

85

ELEGY FOR WONG TOY

Charlie   you are dead now
but I dare to speak because
in China the living speak
to their kindred   dead.
And you are one of my fathers.

Your iron bachelorhood perplexed
our horny youth: we were born
to the snow of a prairie town
to the empty streets of our
longing. You built a railway
                    to get there.

You were your own enduring   winter.
You were your abacus, your Chinaman's
eyes. You were the long reach up
to the top of that bright showcase
where   for a few pennies
we bought a whole childhood.

Only a Christmas calendar
told us your name:
Wong Toy, prop., Canada Cafe:
above the thin pad of months,
under the almost naked girl
in the white leather boots
who was never allowed to undress
in the rows of God-filled houses

which you were never
invited to enter.

Charlie, I knew my first touch
of Ellen Kiefler's young breasts
in the second booth from the back
                         in your cafe.
It was the night of a hockey game.
You were out in the kitchen
making sandwiches and coffee.

87

You were your own enduring
winter.   You were our spring
and we   like meadowlarks
hearing the sun   boom
under the flat horizon
cracked the still dawn alive
with one ferocious   song.

So Charlie   this is a thank-you
poem. You are twenty years
dead. I hope they buried you
sitting upright in your grave
the way you sat   pot-bellied
behind your jawbreakers
and your licorice plugs,
behind your tins of Ogden's fine cut,
your treasury of cigars,

and the heart-shaped box of chocolates
that no-one ever took home.

STONE-HAMMER POEM

1

This stone
become a hammer
of stone, this maul

is the colour
of bone (no,
bone is the colour
of this stone maul).

The rawhide loops
are gone, the
hand is gone, the
buffalo's skull
is gone;

the stone is
shaped like the skull
of a child.

2

This paperweight on my desk

where I begin
this poem   was

found in a wheatfield
lost (this hammer,
this poem).

Cut to a function,
this stone was
(the hand is   gone—

3

Grey, two-headed,
the pemmican maul

fell from the travois or
a boy playing   lost it in
the prairie wool or
a squaw   left it in
the brain of a buffalo or

It is a million
years older than
the hand that
chipped stone or
raised slough
water (or blood) or

4

This stone maul
was found

in the field
my grandfather
thought
was his

my father
thought was his

5

It is a stone
old as the last
Ice Age, the
retreating/the
recreating ice,
the retreating
buffalo, the
retreating Indians

(the saskatoons bloom
white (infrequently
the chokecherries the
highbush cranberries the
pincherries bloom
white along the barbed
wire fence (the
pemmican   winter

91

6

This stone maul
stopped a plow
long enough for one
Gott im Himmel.

The Blackfoot (the
Cree?) not

finding the maul
cursed.

?did he curse
?did he try to
go back
?what happened
I have to/I want
to know (not *know*)
?WHAT HAPPENED

7

The poem
is the stone
chipped and hammered
until it is shaped
like the stone
hammer, the maul.

8

Now the field is
mine because
I gave it
(for a price)

to a young man
(with a growing son)
who did not

notice that the land
did not belong

to the Indian who
gave it to the Queen
(for a price) who
gave it to the CPR

gave it to my grandfather
(for a price) who
gave it to my father
(50 bucks an acre
Gott im Himmel I cut
down all the trees I
picked up all the stones) who

gave it to his son
(who sold it)

9

This won't
surprise you.

My grandfather
lost the stone maul.

10

My father (retired)
grew raspberries.
He dug in his potato patch.
He drank one glass of wine
each morning.
He was lonesome
for death.

He was lonesome for the
hot wind on his face, the smell
of horses, the distant
hum of a threshing machine,
the oilcan he carried, the weight
of a crescent wrench in his hind pocket.

He was lonesome for his absent
son and his daughters,
for his wife, for his own
brothers and sisters and
his own mother and father.
He found the stone maul
on a rockpile in the
northwest corner of what
he thought of
as his wheatfield.

He kept it (the
stone maul) on the railing
of the back porch in
a raspberry basket.

11

I keep it
on my desk
(the stone).
Sometimes I use it
in the (hot) wind
(to hold down paper)

smelling a little of cut
grass or maybe even of
ripening wheat or of
buffalo blood hot
in the dying sun.

Sometimes I write
my poems for that

stone hammer.

F. P. GROVE: THE FINDING

Dreaming the well-born   hobo of yourself
against the bourgeois father   dreaming Europe
if only to find   a place to be from

the hobo tragedian   pitching bundles
riding a freight   to the impossible city
the fallen archangel   of Brandon or Winnipeg

in all your harvesting   real
or imagined   did you really find
four aged stallions   neigh

in your cold undertaking   on those trails north
in all the (dreamed) nights   in stooks
in haystacks   dreaming the purified dreamer

who lured you   to a new man (back
to the fatal earth)   inventing (beyond
America) a new world   did you find

did you dream   the French priest who hauled you
out of your *fleurs du mal*   and headlong
into a hundred drafts   real

or imagined   of the sought form
(there are no models)   and always
(there are only models)   alone

2

alone in the cutter   in the blizzard
two horses   hauling you into the snow
that buries the road   burying the forest

the layered mind   exfoliating
back to the barren sea   (Greek to us,
Grove)   back to the blank sun

and musing snow to yourself   new
to the old rite of burial   the snow
lifting the taught man   into the coyote self

96

the silence of sight   "as if I were not myself
who yet am I"   riding the drifted snow
to your own plummeting   alone and alone

the *wirklichkeit*   of the word itself
the name under the name   the sought
and calamitous edge   of the white earth

the horses   pawing the empty fall
the hot breath on the zero day   the man
seeing the new man so vainly   alone

we say with your waiting wife   (but she
was the world   before you invented it
old liar)   "You had a hard trip?"

97

ELI MANDEL

Born 1922, Estevan, Saskatchewan. Lived in Saskatchewan until he joined the Army Medical Corps in 1943. Studied at the Universities of Saskatchewan and Toronto. He has taught at Collège Militaire Royale, the University of Alberta, and York University, where he is presently Professor of Humanities and English. Editor of several influential anthologies of Canadian literature and criticism. His collection *An Idiot Joy* won the Governor General's Award in 1967. Books: *Trio* (with Gael Turnbull, Phyllis Webb, 1954), *Fuseli Poems* (1960), *Black and Secret Man* (1964), *Criticism: The Silent Speaking Words* (1966), *An Idiot Joy* (1967), *Irving Layton* (1969), *Crusoe* (1973), *Stony Plain* (1973).

ESTEVAN, SASKATCHEWAN

A small town bears the mark of Cain,
Or the oldest brother with the dead king's wife
In a foul relation as viewed by sons,
Lies on the land, squat, producing
Love's queer offspring only,
Which issue drives the young
To feign a summer madness, consort with skulls,
While the farmer's chorus, a Greek harbinger,
Forecasts by frost or rings about the moon
How ill and black the seeds will grow.
This goodly frame, the earth, each of its sons,
With nature as a text, and common theme
The death of fathers, anguished in betrayal
From the first family returns a sacrifice
Of blood's brother, a splintered eyeball
Groined in the fields, scarecrow to crows.
This warns Ophelia to her morning song,
Bawdy as a lyric in a pretty brain gone bad,
While on these fields the stupid harvest lies.

PRAIRIE AS HAWK, COCK, BELLY, LOVER

Hawk beaks his bird in a lost rat.
No squeak unhooks her. Untowned rat
Flies in death. After the bird's beak
In her belly, earth eyes hawk.
Crazed lovers quarrel. Squawk
Earth and hawk: a sunset scrap.
Earth's end a cock's hot trap.

100

FROM THE NORTH SASKATCHEWAN

when on the high bluff discovering
the river cuts below
                              send messages
we have spoken to those on the boats

I am obssessed by the berries they eat
all night odour of Saskatoon
and an unidentifiable odour
something baking
                              the sun
never reaches the lower bank

I cannot read the tree markings

today the sky is torn by wind:
a field after a long battle
strewn with corpses of cloud

give blessings to my children
speak for us to those who sent us here
say we did all that could be done
we have not learned
what lies north of the river
or past those hills that look like beasts

REGINA PAINTERS

Mostly they see it as an abstract
Flat as a canvas slashed by lather
Or a bashed-in metal flower.

Never the single-minded whore
Wearing her badge of customers,
A face like grain
               last harvest
Where the brainless asphalt lies.

102

EDMONTON, 1967

as if by Colville
I mean "hard edge"
stucco   white wall
gravel &
            legs
in one direction shadows
leaning & midget
above the pavement narrows
rapid as the river
                        everything
disappears
            neatness: axiomatic
            houses   here
now gone
            "You are impatient
with poetry" my friend writes
from Iceland

ESTEVAN, 1934

remembering the family we
called breeds   the Roques
their house smelling of urine
my mother's prayers before
the dried fish she cursed
them for their dirtiness their
women I remember too
                              how
seldom they spoke and
they touched one another

even when the sun killed
cattle and rabbis
                      even
in the poisoned slow air
like hunters
                like lizards
they touched   stone
they touched
                  earth

SASKATCHEWAN SURVEYOR

at a correction line
he reads the wind's grammar

rhetoric falls from trees

in a simple sentence of land
a disappointed syntax

NARRATIVE POEM

the point is
the story
        that
one no-one
          told

and yet
        cattle
on lean flanked

land leaning
toward plain

and yet
          shacks
coal fire
despair
        the
barbed wire
wolf willow
river ice

but never
a third act
plotting

end or
even

beginning

land
and long
land
        and
land

SID MARTY

Born 1944, South Shields, England. Came to Canada in 1945 and was raised and educated in Medicine Hat. Studied at Sir George Williams University and the University of Calgary. He has worked as park warden at various parks, including Banff where he is presently posted. Books: *Tumbleweed Harvest* (1973), *Headwaters* (1973).

NOW THAT THE CLOUDS ARE GONE AGAIN

Grandfather sitting across the room
trying to keep from smiling
Weary sodbuster's frame
tapering slender fingers
First time he knew
I could play and sing

And only a month before Grandfather died
Old Uncle Allan who played the fiddle
revealed how the old man played at the dances
barrelhouse organ, in the dirty thirties
While his son was fiddling whisky wild
Laughter rolled out on the winter prairie
in the worst years

Grandad who warned me
long time past
"never knew a good musician
study the law"
A true Canadian
bearing false witness to his talent

So I never told him of my vocation
never sent him my book of poems
thinking he would not understand;
and now, unsure
of the man who handled the organ keys
with calloused fists
a mickey flask in his vest
Homestead blues pounding through religion
ringing true in the thirties wastes:

    "we look away
    across the plains
    and wonder why it never rains
    now that the clouds are gone again"

And he's gone now, has followed his wife
and stillborn children
into the last dark coulee

never played a bar of his music for me

So I'm left with a ragged fiddle
mouldering away in a cold cellar
A bust-up organ gone to seed
in a long-forgotten homestead
drifted in with sand

Left with a rasping melody
my uncle sings, notes that are spindrift
snatched from the dusty teeth
of the plain's wind

A music that comes from the ground
and wounds the hillside yet
Where his sodhouse lingers
tired of years

Now rusty barbed wire
strummed by that inexorable element
And only Coyote, shifting partridge
blends his song in a wild melody
that only wild singers can sing

For the last time I held
those long fingers
I did not know that music
pulsed from blood to blood

The last time I saw
Grandfather
He told me the years were bowing
those wide shoulders
he gave to me

MEDICINE HAT

One time I went back
in a dry month
But all my friends
were gone
from the tumbleweed town
by the brown river

I cannot put the cycle in reverse
The prairie ground
burns slowly dry
as the petrified hills,
leaves this lonely earth

Forecast in a wavering line
of trees, the town grows closer
in the heat haze

The river flows slowly
Broken by the need
of a bottomless sky

Like the river, like the rain
men learn early of need

Macoun wrote to Sandford Fleming
1873; "bunch grass soon dies out
when pastured, and sage brush
takes its place"

No-one heeded his advice,
Sagebrush is the smell of home

Still this land befriends
gophers, coyotes, prairie owls
and man
All who tunnel
water or sweat
into turf

Still, the sun is puzzled
by all pretexts of a town

For only the moon concedes
the roofs of the prairie

113

THE PRAIRIE

Now but a bruise on the sidehill,
the sod hut they packed their love into
Little more than desire
kept out the sun and the rain
Not much more than love
did they have
there on the ravished plain

Here is their hard won house
abandoned now
that they built from the roots
coming out of the ground at last
to name every direction they wheeled in
and plant their landmark in the air,
to break the desolate arc
. . . but the name of the house is lost
like them

It is a secret kept by the neighbours
who survived
the politics of wind
and money

They will understand me
knowing how hard it is
to corral the wind

And you strangers
knowing only the highway,
you too
can at least imagine
in that extremity
as any desert
the sole relief of a tree

Hunting grouse
on the old abandoned farm,
we found a crabapple tree
heavy with fruit,
eaten only by deer

How many years ago
did the couple we'll say
were young
windburnt flowers
plant the dozen varieties
of trees

Act of love, to seed the prairie
among the buffalo beans,
the old dream shouldered aside

Sliced the turf, and watered green shoots
from mountain streams flowing
under deep black dirt
under the glacial debris

A thousand beaded pails
carried in the heat of summer
flashing of the metal
by the white alkali sloughs

Crabapples cured by frost taste sweet
tasting of cool nights
moonshine cider,
water, the depths of earth

The flavour of love savoured by strangers
lingers on in red crabapples
Though the passion of this house
has faded like a fiery old woman
hugging the wind in her spaces
beneath the open windows of the sky

TUMBLEWEED HARVEST

Tumbleweed harvest
under an autumn moon
See how they blow like ghosts
to pile up on barbed-wire fences
and choke the mouths, and the creeks
of the coulee

Late in the year, they catch
the driven snow
make hills and windrows
out on the baldheaded prairie

They pile up in the doorways
of ruined farms
They buffet the unwary walker
harried by wind in the darkness
driving thorns through clothes
which reach the skin

and draw blood

FOX ON THE WIRE

Where did you come from
red one
to dance upended
deadly still
in the south country
of Saskatchewan

A herd of deer
run the edge
of yellow stubble
All around
the purple crocuses
stretch to the Wood Mountain
over spring wet earth

Here on the nuisance ground
flowers bedeck a rusty Ford
old cans full of sweet water
hold the sky, mirror your body

Your coat was prime and full
soft as new snow, red like autumn fire

SASKATCHEWAN AND THE ROCKY MOUNTAINS (1859–1860)

Southesk, casually lighting your meerschaum
and sparking a prairie fire
covering thousands of acres
you said "the conflagration
raged far and wide. I never heard
to what extent it spread. . . ."

How I loved your wanton naïveté
the things you left unsaid
lest you be undone
in literary circles

Your notes on Shakespeare
made while icicles ran
down your nose in a winter tent

Your trigger-happy aspirations
somehow at odds with your careful study
of the prairie chicken *Tetrao Cupido*
(your etymology), now nearly extinct
alas, along with the buffalo grass

and the English aristocracy

JOHN NEWLOVE

Born 1938, Regina, Saskatchewan. Lived for a number of years in Russian farming communities of eastern Saskatchewan, where his mother was a schoolteacher. Has written and worked in many parts of Canada, recently as senior editor for McClelland and Stewart in Toronto. Books: *Grave Sirs* (1962), *Elephants, Mothers and Others* (1963), *Moving in Alone* (1965), *What They Say* (1967), *Black Night Window* (1968), *The Cave* (1970), *Lies* (1972).

118

KAMSACK

Plump eastern Saskatchewan River town,
where even in depression it's said the wheat
went 30 bushels and was full-bodied,
the river laying good black dirt each year:
but I found it arid, as young men will.

119

EAST FROM THE MOUNTAINS

The single, faltering, tenuous line of melody
displayed by a thin man's lungs
unsurely, halting in the winter air:

what to say? Oh, say nothing.
But listen to the blowing snow
at the house's wooden corner,
listen to the misery in the sound of the wind.

On a single wind, followed
by lonely silence, the snow
goes by. Outside
everything is gone: the white
sheer land answers no questions,
but only exists

as it ought to, the sun
shines now as it ought to shine,
shedding no warmth:
what to say.

To listen to the high-pitched wind
in winter removes the idea of hills,
makes clear the real geometry
of the land: east from the mountains
and east to the giant lakes and the river
no single distinction to ruin
the total wholeness of sweep
of the earth, untouched by the lights
of the cold and isolate cities:
following the tentative line
of a gully, it becomes lost at last
as in Qu'Appelle; following
the tentative line of the railway
it gathers together and disappears;
the perspective is textbook,
the rare protruberance never in mind.

The cities do not extend to each other,
the hamlets exist alone,
the suspicious basses of voices
of farmers mutter in the horse-
urined yards, the wives and the children
wait for the spring, summer, fall, the grass,
the quick, unlasting reprieve, gone

like that!—and so hard
to hear what someone is saying:
it is important and real, what is said,
in the thrown-together town,
but is heard from a long way away,
hollow or shrill, and heard
with trouble. So hard

to attend as the issuing words
emerge from an icy tunnel of lung,
faltering tenuous melody—

o tired and halting song!

122

VERIGIN, MOVING IN ALONE,

(fatherless, 250 people
counting dogs and gophers
we would say, Jmaeff's grocerystore,
me in grade 4, mother
principal of the two-building
three-room twelve-grade school,)

a boy sitting on the grass
of a small hill, the hot fall,
speaking no Russian, an airgun
my sister gave me making me envied.

I tried all fall, all spring
the next ominous year, to kill
a crow with it, secretly glad
I could not, the men
in winter shooting the town's
wild dogs, casually tossing
the quick-frozen barely-bleeding
head-shot corpses onto
the street-side snowbanks,

123

the highway crews cutting their way
through to open the road with what
I was sure was simply
some alternate of a golden summer's
wheat-threshing machine, children
running through the hard-tossed spray,
pretending war from the monster's snout,

leaping into snowbanks from
Peter The Lordly Verigin's
palace on the edge of town in
a wild three-dimensional
cubistic game of cops and robbers,

cold spring swimming
in Dead Horse Creek and farmers'
dugouts and doomed fishing
in beastless ponds, strapped
in school for watching a fight,

coldly holding back tears
and digging for drunken father's
rum-bottle, he had finally
arrived, how I loved him,
loved him, love him, dead, still.

My mad old brother chased me
alone in the house with him
around and around
the small living-room, airgun,
rifle in hand, silently,
our breaths coming together—

all sights and temperatures
and remembrances, as
a lost gull screams now
outside my window,
a nine-year-old's year-long
night and day in tiny
magnificent prairie Verigin:

the long grey cat we got,
the bruised knees, cut fingers,
nails in feet, far walks
to watch a horse's corpse
turn slowly and sweetly to bone,
white bone, and in late spring
too, I remember the bright
young bodies of the boys,

my friends and peers and enemies
till everything breaks down.

RIDE OFF ANY HORIZON

Ride off any horizon
and let the measure fall
where it may—

on the hot wheat,
on the dark yellow fields
of wild mustard, the fields

of bad farmers, on the river,
on the dirty river full
of boys and on the throbbing

powerhouse and the low dam
of cheap cement and rocks
boiling with white water,

and on the cows and their powerful
bulls, the heavy tracks
filling with liquid at the edge

of the narrow prairie
river running steadily away.

126

Ride off any horizon
and let the measure fall
where it may—

among the piles of bones
that dot the prairie

in vision and history
(the buffalo and deer,

dead indians, dead settlers
the frames of lost houses

left behind in the dust
of the depression,

dry and profound, that
will come again in the land

and in the spirit, the land
shifting and the minds

blown dry and empty—
I have not seen it! except

in pictures and talk—
but there is the fence

127

covered with dust, laden,
the wrecked house stupidly empty)—

here is a picture for your wallet,
of the beaten farmer and his wife
leaning toward each other—

sadly smiling, and emptied of desire.
*

Ride off any horizon
and let the measure fall
where it may—

off the edge
of the black prairie

as you thought you could fall,
a boy at sunset

not watching the sun
set but watching the black earth,

never-ending they said in school,
round: but you saw it ending,

finished, definite, precise—
visible only miles away.

*

Ride off any horizon
and let the measure fall
where it may—

on a hot night the town
is in the streets—

the boys and girls
are practising against

each other, the men
talk and eye the girls—

the women talk and
eye each other, the indians
play pool: eye on the ball.

*

Ride off any horizon
and let the measure fall
where it may—

129

and damn the troops, the horsemen
are wheeling in the sunshine,
the cree, practising

for their deaths: mr poundmaker,
gentle sweet mr bigbear,
it is not unfortunately

quite enough to be innocent,
it is not enough merely
not to offend—

at times to be born
is enough, to be
in the way is too much—

some colonel otter, some
major-general middleton will
get you, you—

indian. It is no good to say,
I would rather die
at once than be in that place—

though you love that land more,
you will go where they take you.

Ride off any horizon
and let the measure fall—

where it may;
it doesn't have to be

the prairie. It could be
the cold soul of the cities
blown empty by commerce

and desiring commerce
to fill up emptiness.

The streets are full of people.

It is night, the lights
are on; the wind

blows as far as it may. The streets
are dark and full of people.

Their eyes are fixed as far as
they can see beyond each other—

to the concrete horizon, definite,
tall against the mountains,
stopping vision visibly.

THE PRAIRIE

One compiles, piles, piles
these masses of words, verbs,
massifs, mastiffs barking meaning,
dried chips
of buffalo dung, excreta from beasts

the prairie fed, foddered,
food for generations: men roaming
as beasts seen through dips
in history, fostered by legend,
invented remembrance. Scenes shake,

the words do not suffice. One bred
on the same earth wishes himself
something different, the other's
twin, impossible thing, twining
both memories, a double meaning,

but cannot be—never
to be at ease, but always migrating
from city to city
seeking some almost seen
god or food or earth or word.

IF YOU WOULD WALK

One long look down the undulating line of prairie
leads to the horizon; no mountains stop the vision;
the gold fields sway easily.

If you would walk through them,
black clattering birds rising up,
the stiff grain rasping as you pass,

if you would walk,
your body floating like a ghost,
the smallest swirl behind it,

if you would walk that undulation,
seeking the horizon, you would never find it,
even for one long look.

You would return through the swaying fields and rattling birds
to your own known house, of which you are the core,
more easy as you close the rasping door.

133

LIKE A RIVER

And after flowing into the prairie sunset the big plane settled
to earth as though it were contented in this bowl.
The raiders no longer ride over. Their horses are small now,
used for bareback races at country rodeos. Drunks in the hot sun
whoop and bet a dollar at random on Indians.

Before stolen horses were gained from the South, before
the muskets came in the West, before trade-liquor,
Fort Whoop-Up, before a man could own land forever,
himself alone, if he were white, the bands drifted,
small families moved on foot in wintertime.

It is a lonely place for all of us when the snow curls
and we cannot see from house to house,
if there are houses to see. The cities themselves seem fenced,
as if surrounded by wire as farms are, marked off,
concentration camps of the soul.

How many signs must be known, how many curves recalled
to prove the traveller's still on the earth he thinks he is—
not driving by some sudden unnoticed mistake
through Outer Mongolia, the Argentinian pampas,
nearing an unfamiliar, ruined city in Africa?

We wander. It is our way. The people with whom we have no relation
went also, they on regular trails in search of food,
we on highways, railways, in planes, hungry with curiosity,
forgetting as soon as we learn, wanting rest
and ownership, something in which to believe for once.

The plane will go up and on to another separate city
from which the sunset flows like a river into the blackening sky;
we will go on, until we are gone. And on the prairie
the ghosts who own it continue to walk in clans,
searching for food and for what they once knew.

135

PETER STEVENS

Born 1927, Manchester, England. Emigrated to Canada in 1957 teaching school and studying at McMaster. In 1964 he moved to Saskatchewan where he studied and taught at the University of Saskatchewan. From 1968 to 1973 he was poetry editor of *Canadian Forum*. Presently Professor of English at the University of Windsor. Books: *Nothing but Spoons* (1969), *A Few Myths* (1971), *Bread Crusts and Glass* (1972), *Family Feelings* (1974), *Momentary Stay* (1974), *And the Dying Sky Like Blood* (1974).

136

WINTER STORM

A fence strung with wire
sings thin in the wind
sliding small dunes round stumps.

Brown tufts blade-sharp against white
burst in the cold
small detonations of silence
within the screech.

These slide past my eyes
fixed on the road's black grooves
thick parallels
cutting to the horizon's circle—
behind me blue deep as black,
in front blue light dissolving
to a bruise
as the snow lets fly
at the land preserved
in amber drained to ice.

And solid light breaks down to blur
turning my flesh transparent
a sliver of brittle crystal
I
blind at the storm centre.

AFTER THIS MESSAGE

Promises packed
in frail carts
they trundled into the open
wilderness
beached on a wordless continent.

The first huts pushed
out of the dust
and deaths
hardened under snow
locking them into the land
surrounded by the sounding wind
strange whoops and finally
shots drums and smoke
puffing reports
among alien signs
on banners.

This leviathan swallowed
those speechless Jonahs
belched up as bones
these skeletal cities
where frantic pleas
charge along streets
crackle and fizz
petering out
on the wide prairie
howled down by wind
faint and spare
static at the end of the line.

The pulse of our flesh
beats at your ear-drums
as we caper ungainly
singing out of tune
but singing
after a lonely and menaced
apprenticeship of silence.

PRAIRIE: TIME AND PLACE

We can't comprehend the prairie
flattened into need; we feel it
in the cold testing flesh
tight across our skulls
waiting for the ease of greenness
where bunch-topped aspens lean
in the wind's reach for the sky
struggling to trap in their branches
all the wide horizon.

The sun's clear-edged heat
parches minds to dry bone
but we grope for firmness;
we see brush holding on
huddled in blurred clusters.

A single track stitches towns
along straight lines; above them
white names flake from red walls
thrown black across bleached fields.
Trucks bounce over gravel ruts
through their own dust flying
along all the main streets
banked by wind-skinned snow
melting to mud and dust.

A few speculative images
shyly define our place
trying to embrace our world
the necessarily outrageous flats
pitted against the huge sky.

139

PRAIRIE

There is nothing

nothing to stand in
the way of the eye.

Earth rolls under light
scabbed by brush.

Over water course
over slough and sand-flat

eye travels out
to rest on land's ledge.

Sky sheets down
sun-glazed air

eye open
in/to space where

there is nothing.

SASKATCHEWAN

All skylocked, this enormous flatness holds
Like a prehistoric beast a long machine
Angularly unheroic. Waiting, arms up,
Poles are standing at attention, uneasy, thin,
Reaching for the sky, forever on the verge
Of the sharp inevitable crack that never comes.
Ready for an operatic slump to earth,
Some sag, expectant, lean in frozen flight.
Others prop them with invisible wires
To small and kepied heads; an army, weak
And failing in its task, this huge conspiracy.

What vast conspiracy is this? What rebels?
In any case, the sky is winning, strapping down
The edges. There's no escape or hideout, trapped
In its burning mercy, cloudless, still.
When spurting birds flirt in sudden bits
Of blackness on the prairie, they get nowhere
Imprisoned by its size. The sky is really on top.
It's far too big for treason. Who could try
Conspiracy against it and hope to win?

Some, in the secret, seem to be collaborators.
A crow, deliberate and black, stands on the road
Belonging to the car, then in measured scorn
Above the engine's roar rises on its shriek.
Another bird, small and swooping to the car
(In sympathy?) leaves two feathers bristling
On the windshield. Who is right? Derisive crow
Or pitying bird? Their meaning is the same,
Although they teach us different attitudes.
For who are we? We merely are intruders.

It won't do. It's too comforting and neat.
We're at the brittle black edge of the world.
Drive along this road, and an end will come;
Car and you will flip and, spinning, plunge
To some similarity of sky and burn.

The poles have no effect upon this time and space.
Their heroism has no meaning, is a pose.
They are just counters, carriers of mere words,
A lost vocabulary caught in a moment's pulse
Soon gone, although they keep their attitudes
Of nervous supplication. That image of the beast
Is nothing but a cliché dead before it lives;
No prehistoric beasts, this land has swamped them,
And sky is over land. It's no element for birds,
Usurping the road or staying down to earth.
Up there they help the sky in its attack.
There's no defiance, just collusion, studied, bleak.
It's all decided, conclusion logical, foregone.

We'll all drop into deepening well of sky
Which, patronising all at last, will stoop down
And neatly folding all the edges first of all
Will pick the prairie up, to swallow it whole
Like an oyster, curl round itself in surfeit
And forgetting victory for a moment, will consume
Everything—itself, the prairie, all of us
In vicious puff of black and bitter smoke.

143

ON THE EDGE

The city has no myths
and almost no legends.
History is too short-lived
to change to legend.
Living on the edge
of starvation's fact, dust's reality
people create no myths
threatened as they are
by quite authentic devils.

It's not for want of trying.
The river steams—
a touch of hell,
but it's only the power station
pouring waste energy into the water.
No Charon hovers in the stream.
We cross by sleek stone bridges,
Or a black steel bridge
not to hell to forget
but to remember
our necessary maybe vulgar things—
bread, underpants and shoes.

These are the torments we cross to,
the wind eroding flesh to the bone.

Schools take the stance of castles
but we have bred no knights,
no dragons, giants, giant-killers.
The Bessborough rises, grotesque palace
from a bad fairy tale,
replete with formal garden,
yet maybe Hoffman works inside
heating the furnace
to push out smoke
fraying in the winter air
as he makes his clockwork dolls.
Someday they'll stalk out
to take the city from within.

145

Perhaps he'll make some dryads
for the city trees,
their arms whipping down
even breaking with screams
to warn us the legends are coming.
Our dryads are bundled in Siwash sweaters,
heads down against the wind,
intent only on their feet getting there,
not in the process of going.

146

The sod huts have collapsed.
The Indians starve or drink.
Chuckwagons rot or preen themselves
useless in the museum.
We've made the city safe
but we're still uncomfortable,
our buildings bonily bleak
castellated against attack,
the river dourly grey,
willowy girls in fat-sweatered bunches.

147

We think we have cancelled out
all possibilities of myths and legends.
Eyes averted from each other
we die in our waste energy.
The chiefs are waiting outside
ready to take over,
to paddle long canoes through the steam,
elevate Hoffman as a martyr,
pitch their tepees in the formal garden,
feather the girls
or nail them to trees,
carve their totems
and leaving our buildings as bones
invite the buffaloes back
and dance,
let off their own steam,
call up their long dead legends
and worship their gods
surviving in their myths.

148

PRAIRIE POETRY

around us
drifting
crusts the snow
but

later

creation alone

stalks
the land

sometimes lies

with no pattern

swell
to full sound
made neat at ears
strangled
understanding
may yet discover by
questionings

knowing they are

a rawness
fortuitously

greens into crops
which push
under care
wheat
shrivelled
by droughts
is not
steadfast
but somehow
must brace up
to be slashed
and stacked

149

the prairies
assert themselves
in awkward
stone

wheat
moulds
such blank buildings

in the hard glare

ramshackle hovels

persistence
stamps
order

with false fronts
of poetry

in unknowing hands
hopefully
growth
sprouts from earth
with
desperate cities
with elevators
the prairie decays
into one-street towns
that slide away
to vacancy

150

PRAIRIE NEGATIVE

No shore here
gnawed by sea
only thick
horizon lip
level surge
of land broken
by city cliffs.

No gulls here
sweep white
cries raw
above the oil
swell harbour
smell litter;
here birds only
darkly flicker
mute and small
across grey rivers.

No pines here
climb slopes
no slopes here
deep green
in the heat
only aspens
struggle bunched
in clumps
stalk white
in the dust.

151

ANDREW SUKNASKI

Born 1942, Wood Mountain, Saskatchewan. Studied at University of Victoria, Notre Dame (Nelson) and Simon Fraser. Editor of several presses and periodicals dealing with experimental poetry. Describes himself as a migrant worker, presently working in Regina. Books: *The Shadow of Eden Once* (1970), *Four Parts Sand* (with Earle Birney, Judith Copithorne, bill bissett, 1972), *Suicide Notes, Book One* (1973), *Leaving* (1974), *Leaving Wood Mountain* (1975), *Wood Mountain Poems* (1976).

LANTERNS

the blizzard came
after the first frost—
the hired man left the house
with a lantern
to see how the cattle
were taking the storm
in the north pasture

my father found him
three days later
near the fence on the east side
of the pasture

the faithful dog froze
beside him—curled up
like a lover in the man's arms
(the broken lantern
lay near a stone   the glass shattered)

men freeze this way everywhere
when lanterns fall   a p a r t
(even within one's arms
inside the city's rim)

DEATHLOCKS

for sid marty

winter moves down
from the mountains—
last night frost flamed
the larches into orange

this morning
on the trail into boom lake
cold wind curves my scent
into nostrils of two bull elk
facing one another
in a meadow

the elk briefly glance
my way
& then begin to spar—
i listen to faint clicking sounds
of antlers
till the elk cease
their playful sparring
(it will grow more serious
in a week or two)

154

as the elk graze a while
& then face one another
something brings to mind pale images
of two farmers i saw fight once
at a dance in a prairie school
(i remember the look of melancholy
in their eyes
before the frost of hate
flamed their faces red—
the sound of cracking bones
as their fierce arms locked
while a young girl cried
in the forest of people
surrounding them)

155

SASKATCHEWAN POTASH MINE

i'm going to see my brother
who works at the mine near rockenville
i said to the manitoba miner
as he picked me up near the boundary—
he talked about a deer he shot
in the fall near the budding willows
that seemed to stitch the sky
to the prairie at the horizon

as we parked in the lot by the mine
he pointed to the guard at the gate—
said the man would be able to tell me
when my brother's shift was through

the guard pointed out my brother's car—
said i could meet him there in a few hours
(it began to drizzle as i walked
over to a vein of poplars & willows
to shelter myself as the wind rose—
growing colder   i began to curse
the guard the mine & fence
topped with barbwire—i muttered:
goddamn concentration camp!

what kind of people work here?
relentlessly walking to keep warm
i found a deer antler with a deep mark
gouged across the thickest part—
later when i met my brother at the car
he looked at the marked antler & laughed:
that's one buck that got away—
the bullet merely grazed the antler)

on our way to rockenville
we stopped at the edge of the village
where an approach road joins the highway
to the graveyard—
my brother pointed out faint tire-marks
where a car hit a culvert deadcentre
(he said the young miner from the late shift
must have fallen asleep
& that it must have happened at dawn
because another miner going to the morning shift
found him—
my brother pointed to the man's house
across the road   & said: that's where he lived
he was so close to home—
today at the mine we all signed away a day's pay
to his wife & children   900 of us)

157

TEO'S BAKERY

the time is spring in central manitoba
& already the sun is baking
flourwhite breasts of women

today i'm happy
& sing an old frenchcanadian song for teo
as he stands behind the bakery
wondering who the hell this joker is
(some crazy bugger singing
to garbage cans all afternoon
as if they were angels—
or maybe even girls)

& teo's kind of happy too now
because he remembers this funny monk song
which he sang in his youth
(of course teo's kinda high—
which helps him enjoy the song)

158

hours later
teo dressed in white like a priest
goes on the night shift
in his bakery that feeds a village
& the whole countryside
walking tonight
lonely as judas i stop to watch teo
thru the bakery window
as he kneads dough like watered-down visions
of childhood   suddenly
he reaches for something under the huge table—
my God! teo!   a crock of wine—
wine red as the sun pouring its warmth
across the other side of this hungry world—

then i nod   smiling as teo wipes the sweat
or tears from his face
because it's hot as hell
near that leviathan of a brick oven
(& i've just been talking with a villager
who says things aren't going too well for teo
& his wife   & that the only son
refuses to take the bakery over)

159

HOMESTEAD/1914/SEC 32/TP 4/RGE 2/W 3RD

for andrew suknaski sr.

for the third spring in a row
i return to visit my father

the first time
i hadn't seen him for eleven years—
he was a bit spooked when he first saw me
as he stood there with a binder-twine
holding up his old wool pants
(he wore an ole army sweater
he'd sewn himself into months ago)
he embraced me & kissed me

anyway
that year he was still a fairly tough lil bugger
& we shouted to the storm as we fought
to see who'd carry my flightbag
across the cn tracks of yorkton—me crying:
for chrissake Father!
lemme carry the damn thing—
the train's already too close!

but now in his 83rd year
father fails (is only 1 10 pounds now)—
he cries as he tells me about his growing pain
after the fall from a cn freightcar—
says his left testicle has shriveled up
to the size of a walnut—
he says there's no fuckin way
he's going to see another doctor
(the last one tried to slip a penlight
up the ole man's ass—sez father:
no-one's ever looked up my ass & never will)

father walks me through a spring storm
to the bus depot—
he is bent even more now   thin as a grasshopper
& i think. . .
we'll have to break the ole man's back
to lay him flat when he dies

161

as he guards my bag in the depot
i buy two white owl cigars in the cafe
& return to give him one—
we embrace as we say goodbye—
& i watch him disappear in the snowflake eddy
around the pine on the street corner—
remembering how he stood under a single lightbulb
hanging from a frayed wire in his shack
& said: my life now moves to an end
          with the speed of electricity

THE ELEVATOR AGENT

for johnny soparlo

three elevators
on edge
of wood mountain
& his
the last
west one
bisecting
the north south
road allowance

remembering
boyhood story
of one who
is reported
to have been
saved
long ago
to ascend darkness
with the other
two

163

or so we are
told
by one witness
in the book

remembering
the three
hungry
froshog boys
how we
picked beer bottles
around the
elevator
the rare green
bottle
something to
treasure
if ever found

164

often watching
the elevator agent
on rope lift
the way
he mysteriously
disappeared
high into darkness
to later
return
from a place
we could never
see

watching him
dust around
eyes
dust fine
& delicately
encrusted
as wings
of dry moth
once shaken from
a green bottle.

165

MIRIAM WADDINGTON

Born 1917, Winnipeg, Manitoba. Studied at the University of Toronto and the Pennsylvania School of Social Work in Philadelphia. After a career as a social worker she became a teacher of English, and now teaches at York University. Books: *Green World* (1945), *The Second Silence* (1955), *The Season's Lovers* (1958), *The Glass Trumpet* (1966), *Call Them Canadians* (1968), *Say Yes* (1969), *A. M. Klein* (1970), *Driving Home: Poems New and Selected* (1972), *The Price of Gold* (1976).

166

SORROW SONG

I hear a prairie
singing in the house
of summer   the wind
is blowing   the
riders are riding
the wind is sing-
ing a lament for
summer   cold as the
snow   a song fills
the prairie and
words are falling
caught in the grasses
in a desert of dark-
ness where horses
are riding through
oceans of lostness.

The air is cold
in the house of my
summer   the prairie
is singing   the
prairie is turning
and countless the
riders are sound-
lessly singing the
lament of summer the
burial of summer
and the lost house
in the prairie   last
in the distance
sings a song for
the evening   for the
empty spaces   far
away in the darkness.

167

UKRAINIAN CHURCH

Little father your
rhythmic black robe
against white snow
improvises you
a black note
on a white keyboard

let me follow
into your churchbarn
through the gate
to the onion domes
where your carrot
harvest burns
a fire of candles

let me follow
in the cool light
as you move through
God's storehouse
as you put the bins
in order as you set
each grain in place

let me follow
as your voice
moves through the
familiar liturgy
to the low caves
of Gregorian chant
and let me hear
little father

how you pray
for all your geese
for the cow fertile
at Easter   and the
foundations of new
houses to be strong
and firmly set

and let me hear
how you beseech
for all your people
a clear road   an
open gate and
a new snowfall
fresh   dazzling
white as birchbark

WAITING IN ALBERTA

I am sitting in
a very remote
vast faraway
corner of Alberta,
the fourth corner
to be exact   and
although it is
June the snow is
flying but I know
it is only summer
snow and will be
over in an hour
so I make myself
comfortable   fold
a triangle of
lawn over my lap
a few foothills
over my shoulders

put on my bifocals
plug in the heating
pad and though I
know it will even-
tually kill me
I light a cigar-
ette and I watch
the first buildings
go up   then all
the lights go on
they look like
frozen grapes in
the garden of Eden
or like glass fruits
hung on tall motion-
less trees but the
air is clear as
water   not like in
Toronto;

169

And I think from
my very remote
corner of Alberta
that after all this
is a pretty clever
miraculous world
where I can sit
small as anything
in such a big corner
of it and the only
archaic creatures
are us people   every-
thing else is so
up-to-date   buildings
plug-ins   programming
for everything except
us people who can
still even make
love in the old

style if we feel
like it   but I like
just sitting here
with the lawn on
my lap waiting for
the sun to come
out so the orange
prairie poppies
can unwilt and
hold their heads
up again   and the
winds can go to
sleep   and I can
get on with my work.

THINGS OF THE WORLD

A north Winnipeg girl
bending over water
she spent her summers at a lake
and watched the goldeye swim.

Later in the neon season
of an eastern city
she ate its white flesh
off the spiced rainbow skin.

The good things of the world
she learned long ago
from the sun   out there
in the prairies   in that light

Caught frogs and birds
picked hazelnuts and found
lady's slipper in a leafy ditch,
skull-and-cross-boned trees.

171

She played with Indian children
across the river in the saint
settlements and was converted
by the golden statues

To a blazing innocence
easy to learn   but the other
things that harmed her
(even herself)   those
she could never explain.

172

NIGHT OF VOICES

I loved your name   I touched
its ancient deeps and sank
from desert to dividing waters;
darkness drowned the dawn and
your blind touch was a cradle
that I remembered and your name
was blessed and garlanded with
lingering fire and Egyptian snows.

Your mouth tasted of white lilac
and water plants and outside the
grass stood high and the wind
blew down the gravelled roads
of summer; from far away I heard
police cars sirening the suburbs
or was it the watchman calling
across the dusty building lots?
We live in murdered cities   all
locked in pyramids but to your

mountain name I came and saw
anew as through a wall of glass:

your kisses sang of Polish villages
destroyed and built again   of parents'
doubled partings, like one entranced
I stood and looked across my father's
rivers and heard my mother's windmills
in my blood, almost I felt her fears,
almost I heard my uncle's cry against
the burning droughted prairie and

the flooding night was filled with
voices   I heard those secret words
my hands touched out against your face,
day held back from coming and the
silence spoke your storied name above
the droughted prairie and blessed me
with its wheat   touched me with its
root   and fed me grainy light.

But somewhere in darkness
the windmills still await me, the
crying rivers call   the villages are
silent   the watchman merely dozes:
and having called them up
I cannot sleep so lightly or
having known your touch
so easily fare well.

A MAN IS WALKING

A man is walking toward me
With leaning green rhythms
the sky falls away   shoulders
him like a green hood.

The man looks familiar
as he comes closer   I see
that it is my father and
he is bringing me flowers

not ordinary flowers
but a whole tree of them
torn up by the roots
dripping with the blood

of earth with the earth
of his grave in the green
graveyard; and on this day
he arose to bring me flowers

175

and I am startled   imagine him
bringing me flowers and speaking
my name with the old melancholy
shaking his head and saying:

your poems daughter are dark
very dark, there is too much
darkness in the world, go and
plant these broken roots

in the garden and hurry now
they are lythrum   fireweed
remember how you saw them
growing wild every summer

on the way to Gimli   hurry
now and plant them   we have such
drying winds on the prairie such
drying winds in the graveyard.

176

My father is walking toward
me with green rhythms   my
father is bringing me flowers
to plant and he is saying

just as he used to say   there
will be no more cruelty
no more death no more dark
words: for you there will be

only rivers rivers   the
timeless green of rivers
moving and singing their
fertile song in your ears.

177

TRANSFORMATIONS

The blood of my ancestors
has died in me
I have forsaken the steppes
of Russia for the prairies
of Winnipeg, I have turned
my back on Minneapolis
and the Detroit lakes
I love only St. Boniface
its grey wooden churches
I want to spend my life
in Gimli listening to the
roar of emptiness in the
wild snow, scanning the lake
for the music of rainbow-
skinned fishes, I will compose
my songs to gold-eye tunes
send them across the land
in smoke-spaces, ice-signals
and concentrate all winter
on Henry Hudson adrift
in a boat, when he comes home
I will come home too and
the blood of my ancestors
will flower on Mennonite bushes

PROVINCIAL

My childhood
was full of people
with Russian accents
who came from
Humble Saskatchewan
or who lived in Regina
and sometimes
visited Winnipeg
to bring regards
from their frozen
snowqueen city.

In those days
all the streetcars
in the world slept
in the Elmwood
car-barns and the
Indian moundbuilders
were still wigwammed
across the river
with the birds
who sang in the bushes
of St. Vital.

Since then I have
visited Paris
Moscow London
and Mexico City
I saw golden roofs
onion domes and the
most marvellous
canals, I saw people
sunning themselves
in Luxembourg Gardens
and on a London parkbench
I sat beside a man
who wore navy blue socks
and navy blue shoes
to match.

All kinds of miracles:
but I would not trade
any of them for the
empty spaces, the
snowblurred geography
of my childhood.

DALE ZIEROTH

Born 1946, Neepawa, Manitoba. Lived on the prairies until 1968 when he moved to Toronto. Has taught high school, worked in the free school movement and in assorted other jobs. Presently lives in the British Columbia interior. Books: *Mindscapes* (with Paulette Jiles, Susan Musgrave, Tom Wayman, 1971), *Clearing* (1973).

PRAIRIE GRADE SCHOOL

Even now, we entered quietly, afraid
to interrupt and wondering about the
unlocked door. Later we would speak of
the broken water cooler, covered with dust
and the tracks of mice, of the word
scratched with a nail on the blackboard, of
the smell of damp earth and rot. We had
almost expected this. Still, no-one
would mention how we were surprised not so much
by the dead meadowlark in the broken window
as by its silence. . .

In this room, it is easy to remember
the broken legs, the new swear words, the
election of Louis St. Laurent. Here we sat
in rows, memorizing rules that were intended
to last for life; our teachers, young ladies
from Neepawa or bigger towns a great distance away,
always to the south. I was here on the day
things first changed, the day I hid from friends
who learned to play without me, discovering
I controlled nothing and growing afraid
for the first time of ordinary trees. . .

From the distance of less than a mile,
nothing seems changed. The building,
standing at a crossroads (one road
goes nowhere, another the only road
to the last farmer before the bush begins),
still colonizes the half acre of land
seven immigrant fathers and a municipal clerk
stole from the prairie. It remains,
useful only as landmark. And landmark
to none but the homecoming sons of farmers.

182

MANITOBA POEM

In Manitoba, a farmer will prepare
for spring and contrary to popular notion
women are not foremost in men's
minds: the new warmth has made them
aware of trains and hills, of things
that would make them leave women completely:
something else keeps them. And the women
are just as glad for the rest.

Summer comes in from Saskatchewan on
a hot and rolling wind. Faces
burnt and forearms burnt, the men seed
their separate earths and listen to the CBC
for any new report of rain. Each day now
the sun is bigger and from the kitchen
window, it sets a mere hundred feet behind
the barn, where a rainbow once came down.

Four months later this is over, men
are finished. Children return
to school and catch colds in their
open jackets. Women prepare
for long nights under six-inch goosedown
quilts. Outside, the trees shake off
their leaves as if angered by the new
colours. And without any more warning than
this, winter falls on the world,
taking no-one by surprise. No-one.

184

GLENELLA, MANITOBA

The village, east of highway 5
huddles by the only railway tracks in
50 miles. One white grain elevator
tells you where you are, from any
direction. After four fires the place
is still big enough to have the
usual buildings: school, hall,
station, hotel and two stores.
Sunday evenings, a passenger
train; Thursday, a freight.
There are no factories here
and no luxuries. On two sides
there are hay fields and country;
machinery and men sometimes move
there. North of here is nothing.

185

On Saturday night there are Indians
sick in the pub and Crazy John sitting
in the poolhall where he's sat for years
watching the spinning balls, the young men,
who knows what. Visitors soon discover
there are some here who like
what they have lived through. Mostly, there
are young men who stand waiting
with their hands made fists in
pockets that are empty, young men
who know that Winnipeg
(200 miles south and not big enough
for a place on the map of the world
in the post office), that Winnipeg
is where the world begins.

186

My grandfather came here years ago,
family of eight. In the village,
nine miles away, they knew him as
the German and they were suspicious, being
already settled. Later he was
somewhat liked; still later
forgotten. In winter everything
went white as buffalo bones and
the underwear froze on the line
like corpses. Often the youngest
was sick. Still he never thought
of leaving. Spring was always greener
than he'd known and summer had
kid-high grass with sunsets big
as God. The wheat was thick,
the log house chinked and warm.

187

The little English he spoke
he learned from the thin grey lady
in the one-room school, an hour away
by foot. The oldest could hunt, the youngest
could read. They knew nothing of
the world he'd left, and forgotten,
until 1914 made him an alien and
he left them on the land he'd come to,
120 miles north of Winnipeg.

DETENTION CAMP, BRANDON MANITOBA

On the morning of the fourth day,
two men were missing. Later, brought
back, they talked for a while
of some part of summer they'd seen,
then they were quiet, turned bitter,
even a little crazed: these received
no letters from the outside and spoke now
of nothing they wished to return to.
Bodies at night would moan, asleep
with others somewhere who dreamt
of them. The sunrise on the wall
became a condition, the sunset a way
of counting days. The prisoners carried
these things close to their bodies.
This my grandfather came to know
before leaving.

189

He did not celebrate his homecoming.
His wife was older, his children
came to him less. Even the sky
was not as blue as he'd remembered,
and the harvest, three-quarters done,
reminded him too often of wasted
time, of war in Europe. Winter
came too quickly that year and
next spring the turning of the earth
held no new surprises.

190

FATHER

Twice he took me in his hands and shook
me like a sheaf of wheat, the way a dog shakes
a snake, as if he meant to knock out my tongue
and grind it under his heel right there
on the kitchen floor. I never remembered
what he said or the warnings he gave; she
always told me afterward, when he
had left and I had stopped my crying. I
was eleven that year and for seven more years
I watched his friends laughing and him
with his great hands rising and falling
with every laugh, smashing down on his knees
and making the noise of a tree when it cracks
in winter. Together they drank chokecherry
wine and talked of the dead friends and the
old times when they were young, and because
I never thought of getting old, their
youth was the first I knew of dying.

Sunday before church he would trim
his fingernails with the hunting knife
his East German cousins had sent, the same
knife he used for castrating pigs and
skinning deer: things that had nothing
to do with Sunday. Communion once
a month, a shave every third day, a
good chew of snuff, these were the things
that helped a man to stand in the sun for
eight hours a day, to sweat through each
cold hailstorm without a word, to freeze
fingers and feet to cut wood in winter, to do
the work that bent his back a little more
each day down toward the ground.

Last Christmas, for the first time, he
gave presents, unwrapped and bought
with pension money. He drinks mostly coffee
now, sleeping late and shaving every day.
Even the hands have changed: white, soft,
unused hands. Still he seems content
to be this old, to be sleeping in the middle
of the afternoon with his mouth open as if there
is no further need for secrets, as if he is
no longer afraid to call his children fools
for finding different answers, different lives.

DRIVING TO LETHBRIDGE

For Peter and Liz

Slowly the mountains are coming down
trees seem to reach
higher than before although
they are stunted in deference to the
wind, but then
even at 60 miles an hour there is a point
that is suddenly
all prairie
and it feels like a homecoming
all horizon and clouds
and friends ahead.

After the Frank Slide
you needed something that would
open up like this, take your mind off
the jeezly forces that have pushed you up and down hills
through the rain and water seeping into your car
and into the back of your mind.

After the Crow's Nest, you are
    tired of riding this
    backbone of half death, half life,
needing this great flat land
    dipping in and out of coulees
    where the shrubs grow like hair
and the rivers are slow and wide and blue
    as if they carried the sky.
Homecoming! you can stop the car and
    touch it. Clouds heading east
    blowing across nothing, touching
                nothing. Everyone knows
the mountains are beautiful although they are
    so easy, it takes a God's eye or an Indian's
    to see this place is
        the first room of the universe
        the way it was even before
        the first birth
    Or Lethbridge, growing like a
    stone out of the ground,
a collection of houses and souls hanging together
    against the wind, saving themselves

and their roots. You will never understand
    why the wind has not
        broken it off
        flung it against the barbed wire,
  why it is something the earth
    will never release. Yet your friends
    celebrate any occasion as if to prove
        there doesn't have to be a reason
    to live here. And still
the most interesting history here is
        the Indian's.

The road back is constantly rising and the wind
    from the mountains warns you
        that what is ahead
    gives no second chance. The final turn
        is just ahead, soon
there will be mountains everywhere, rising everywhere
    like cathedrals. You get
    one look back and that is too late: there is only
        mountains now, only
    the sight of yellow leaves
    caught for life on the green spruce boughs.

On the trail to the top of the world
the smell of the earth comes,
clover, water,
the cracked ground or
apples turning their hot faces to the
sun, it comes, opening inside you
like the first flower of earth until there is no
world like this one, no trees or sky
like these although you suspect
the potential for terror anyway
as you would anticipate
a storm.

But you go toward it
despite the reluctance and the fear
you go toward it any way you can, past
the tremors and the
false signposts, there is
a centre that attracts you and you find it
suddenly: the opening into
an organized life, a
world you fit into
perfectly, as water in a river,
child in the womb.

196

And you cannot believe
　　it has always been here;
　it is all here, the agreements and the
　good examples the company of love, you are
　　　the child you were
　　　　the old man you will become, it is
earth without end: where you live no matter
where you are, now that you have left the never-ending trail,
　　now that you have gone through the last stand
　　　of words and things
　　and seen the beautiful green light at the
　　edge of the clearing that is this country's
　　　first promise of home.

197

ACKNOWLEDGEMENTS

Poems by Douglas Barbour are reproduced by permission of the author; poems by George Bowering from *Rocky Mountain Foot* by permission of McClelland and Stewart Limited; poems by Elizabeth Brewster from *Sunrise North* by permission of Clarke, Irwin & Company Limited; poems by Gary Geddes by permission of the author; poems by Robert Kroetsch by permission of Oolichan Books and New Press; poems by Eli Mandel from *Black and Secret Man* by permission of McGraw-Hill Ryerson Limited, from *An Idiot Joy* by permission of Hurtig Publishers, the others by permission of the author. Poems by Sid Marty from *Tumbleweed Harvest* are reproduced by permission of Sundog Press, from *Headwaters* by permission of McClelland and Stewart Limited; poems by John Newlove from *Black Night Window*, *The Cave* and *Lies* by permission of McClelland and Stewart Limited, from *Moving in Alone* by permission of the author; poems by Peter Stevens by permission of the author and Talonbooks; poems by Andrew Suknaski by permission of the author; poems by Miriam Waddington from *Driving Home* by permission of Oxford University Press, the others by permission of the author; poems by Dale Zieroth by permission of House of Anansi Press and the author.

198